FRANCIS SCOTT KEY:
God's Courageous Composer

. . . as we were leaving the enemy flagship a British officer hurried up to us.

"I'm sorry gentlemen," he said firmly. "We are about to attack Baltimore. You must remain with us until the battle is over and the city has surrendered."

I swallowed deeply. I felt as if this were a bad dream, a horrible nightmare from which I would soon awaken.

Colonel Skinner cast a comforting arm around my shoulder. His eyes were misty.

"I know what you're feeling, my friend; but there is nothing we can do."

". . . nothing we can do." The words struck a familiar chord in my memory. I brought back a vision of Grandmother Key as I read to her from the Bible.

"Well, Francis, it is raining outside. You cannot go out and play. There is nothing you can do about it. But we can always pray together. Remember, Francis, you can always pray."

So, on that night of September 13, 1814, I stood on board the ship Minden in the Chesapeake Bay and prayed.

I took an old envelope from my pocket and scribbled a few words and phrases as the battle for Fort McHenry, and the fate of our new nation began. My head pounded with the sound of exploding cannon shots and shells.

I paced along the deck, aware that I was surrounded by hostile sailors. They were hoping for the fort to fall as strongly as I was hoping it would hold.

Without warning the firing stopped. The air was still. How I longed to see the fort. Was the flag still flying?

"Doctor Beane, quickly stumbling to the deck, asked: "Has the fort surrendered?"

"We don't know," I answered. "We can't know until sunrise."

Time crawled. We stood waiting in the darkness.

"The sun is coming up," Colonel Skinner shouted. "The dawn is breaking!"

Once more I took out my envelopes. I scribbled away, noting the glow of the dawn's early light. The mist had cleared the smoke away.

"I can see it!" I exclaimed. "The flag—our flag—it's still there!"

This volume of FRANCIS SCOTT KEY: GOD'S COURAGEOUS COMPOSER, joins a collection of inspiring biographies written by one of America's foremost authors of childrens literature - David R. Collins.

Among his other works are: ABRAHAM LINCOLN: GOD'S LEADER FOR A NATION, GEORGE WASHINGTON CARVER: MAN'S SLAVE BECOMES GOD'S SCIENTIST, HARRY S. TRUMAN, LINDA RICHARDS, and CHARLES AUGUSTUS LINDBERGH, JR.

"I choose subjects who have had a strong Christian influence in their lives," states Collins. "This influence led them to serve other people and make a better world for all of us."

David R. Collins is an English instructor at Woodrow Wilson Junior High School in Moline, Illinois. He earned his Bachelor of Science and Master of Science degrees from Western Illinois University.

In 1975 David Collins was named "Outstanding Educator" by the Illinois Office of Education.

In Moline, Collins maintains a busy schedule of church, civic and educational activities. He is a popular speaker and frequently appears at national writers conferences.

Francis Scott Key

God's Courageous Composer

by

DAVID R. COLLINS

Illustrated by **Joe Van Severen**

MOTT MEDIA

Milford, Michigan 48042

This book
is for my mother
whose life was a song
of
faith and inspiration.

All Scriptures are from the King James Version of the Bible.

COPYRIGHT © 1982 by Mott Media

Robert F. Burkett, Editor

LIBRARY OF CONGRESS CATALOGING IN PUBLICATION DATA

Collins, David R.
    Francis Scott Key: God's Courageous Composer.

    (The Sowers)
    Bibliography: p. 111
    Includes index.

    SUMMARY: The story of an American patriot during the War of 1812 and how his Lord and Savior, Jesus Christ, used him to pen the words which became America's national anthem.
    1. Title. 2. National Anthem. 3. American biographies. 4. Christian heroes.

ISBN 0-915134-91-8 Paperbound

ISBN 0-915134-66-7 Hardbound

FOREWORD

O say can you see by the dawn's early light
What so proudly we hail'd at the twilight's last
*   gleaming . . .*

What American does not thrill to the powerful
words of our own National Anthem? As children we
learn "The Star Spangled Banner" which expresses
our allegiance to our country; and we sing it many
times throughout our lives.

Yet what do we know of the man who gave us these
inspiring words? Most of us know only a name—
Francis Scott Key. Most of us know that he wrote the
words while being held prisoner aboard a ship on the
Chesapeake Bay during the War of 1812. The sight
of the American flag flying above a fort under pro-
longed attack provided the inspiration to Key.

But there was much more to this man than the
words to one song. As a child, Francis Scott Key
learned the Bible. He grew to manhood with a strong
Christian faith guiding his actions and thoughts. Yes,
there were many times of trouble and concern. Always
Key turned to the Lord for guidance, comfort and
direction.

Lord, with glowing heart I'd praise thee
For the bliss thy love bestows,
For the pardoning grace that saves me
And the peace that from it flows . . .

Francis Scott Key constantly offered his thanks by
writing hymns of prayer. His thoughts have become
a part of our spiritual, musical and patriotic heritage.

As you learn of the life of Francis Scott Key, you
begin to appreciate the fact that this man should be

remembered for much more than writing the words to one song. The life of Francis Scott Key was lived in service to God. This story of Key is written as Key himself might have written it. Hopefully the reader may share his experiences in a more personal way.

Key's deep faith stayed with him until the end. In his final weeks, this noble Christian longed for the future promised by his Savior:

"I have been a base and groveling thing,
And the dust of earth my home,
But now that I know the end of my woe,
And the day of my bliss is come.
Then let them like me, make ready their shrouds
Nor shrink from the mortal strife,
And like me they shall sing,
As to heaven they spring,
Death is not the end of life."

Francis Scott Key sowed seeds of faith to his family and friends all his life. The beauty of his words and the example of his Christian life allow us to appreciate him today.

David R. Collins
Moline, Illinois

CONTENTS

Midnight Stranger

"I think I see a living beet
Red from head to dusty feet,
A jump in the creek just might assist her
And reveal to all that it is Ann, my sister!"

I stood smiling, eager to see what reaction my verse would bring from my seven-year-old sister. For a moment, she appeared to be pouting. What a fool I was to think she would have no response. Her eyes flashed mischief and her lips curled in a devilish grin.

"Look at the curls on my brother Frank
Each one of them I'd love to yank!"

The curls, always the curls. No matter how I teased my sister, she would always remind me of my horrid curly hair. How many times had I begged Papa and Mama to let me have my curls cut off?

"But they are handsome," Mama always replied.

"And they are a family sign," Papa would declare.

Well, they were *NOT* handsome to me. The fact that other members of the Key family shared the same affliction brought me little happiness . . . nor did my sister's constant teasing about them. But for this moment, I could not be angry. The sight of my sister looking like a live reddish ball amused me. I knew the redness well. It was the color of our plantation soil. Our family home spread across three thousand acres of fertile valleys in Frederick Country, Maryland. It was called Terra Rubra because of the red earth. In truth, the dirt had an orange shade to it as well. The summer sun and the dust of Terra Rubra had combined to cover my sister in a soft red glow.

"Am I really a terrible sight?" Ann asked meekly.

I nodded. "The cook might easily mistake you for a beet, a tomato, or a carrot."

"All right, Francis Scott Key!" my sister exclaimed. "I have seen you look just as frightful. You needn't carry on so about me!"

"But when I look as frightful, I do not stay dirty long. Have Sarah bring you soap and water. See if that outside covering will come off."

With that, my sister scampered into the house.

"She forgot about you completely, didn't she, General?"

Our woeful-looking shepherd dog stood at the bottom of the front porch stairs. He, too, carried the reddish coating of Terra Rubra on his fur . . . but he stood tall and proud. Papa had named the spirited animal after General Washington with whom he had fought during the days of the Revolutionary War. Since I was born August 9, 1779, I had only heard stories of those exciting days when America won its freedom from England. How I wished I might have carried a musket and fought beside General Washington like my father.

But although Papa was proud of having served his country, he often expressed sorrow that there had been any fighting at all. His own grandfather, Phillip Key, had come from England in 1720.

"It is sad that we had to fight the country from which our own forefathers had come," Papa said.

Mama agreed. "Wisdom is better than weapons of war," she said softly. "It is written in Ecclesiastes 9:18."

Mama often shared wise words from the Bible. As I plopped down on the porch steps to pet General, I tried to remember when mama did not have her Bible nearby. I couldn't. Ann and I both had learned to read and write from the Bible. Its words were our text for learning and its lessons were our rules for living.

"Whatsoever things were written aforetime were written for our learning," said Mama, "that we through patience and comfort of the Scriptures might have hope. That is from Romans 15:4."

Suddenly, there came a loud shout from the south side of the house. General's ears sprang up. I jumped to my feet.

"Hold on, you little varmint!"

I knew that voice at once. It was Peter, one of our slaves and my favorite companion. He came running on the heels of a yelping pig onto the front lawn.

"Stop, stop, you curly-tailed beast!"

I couldn't help but laugh at Peter. He was all arms and legs. I bounded off the stairs, trying to block the path of the fleeing animal. When the pig stopped short, I jumped forward and caught the squirming creature in my arms . . . but in a moment he slipped away.

"I think he knows he's a-headed for the smokehouse!" yelled Peter.

"Then I can't blame him for running!" I hollered back.

Across the flowerbeds the pig raced, pausing now and then behind bushes to catch his breath. Peter and

I crept around on tiptoes, hoping to corner the animal. Just when we got a few steps away, off he darted again. Finally, he scampered behind the house.

Unfortunately, the area in back of the house offered many more places to hide. The pig raced around the stables, the vegetable and fruit storehouses, and the cabin where Mama went to weave and sew.

"You'll never catch him!" called out Alfred, our family blacksmith as we ran in front of his barn. "Two young lads are no match for a loose pig."

Alfred's statement proved to be true enough. After an hour of chasing, the pig still remained free. My clothes were soaked in sweat, and my sides ached from running.

"Let's forget this animal, Peter," I suggested. "Pipe Creek is calling to us."

Peter smiled. He was happy to give up the tiring run-about. The slaves on our plantation were bound to serve the Key family. My suggestion of a swim was a service Peter delighted in joining.

"Yes, Master Francis," he answered. "I do believe I hear the call of Pipe Creek myself."

If ever there was a cool place in which to enjoy life during the summer, it was in the fresh water of Big Pipe Creek. That afternoon in 1789 was like so many others I remember. For hours, Peter and I splashed and swam in the creek.

After the swim, Peter and I borrowed two horses from the stable. We rode bareback across Terra Rubra. Rich plots of corn and tobacco stood sturdy and proud in the late afternoon sun. Light breezes rippled wide waves of wheat. We shouted greetings to the field workers, then spirited our horses onward.

It was sunset by the time we returned home. Peter dashed away to join his family who lived in the far corner of our plantation. Quickly I washed and changed clothes for supper. Papa had little use for stragglers at mealtime.

"If one listens to his stomach, he can judge when it is time to eat," Papa said often. "Tardiness at mealtime is both a nuisance and inconvenience to others waiting to eat. It is reason enough for punishment."

A slight smile always curled Mama's mouth when Papa talked so. I suspect she felt Papa sometimes enjoyed the sound of his own words. He was a judge who rode on horseback from courthouse to courthouse, administering laws fairly. I am certain he was a good judge, but I know he was not always a man of few words. He liked to talk. Ann and I learned to listen. Dinnertime was set aside for Papa's stories. He never seemed to tell the same one twice.

As soon as the meal was over, Mama looked at Ann and me. "I hope both of you will come with me tonight. The people want me to come read to them. They're going to build a fire near the old timbers.''

''I'll come!'' Ann exclaimed.

''So will I!'' I added.

Mama always called our slaves ''the people.'' They were our own special family. Sometimes when our neighbors came to dinner, they talked about their slaves.

''They're not worth the food to feed them!'' I remember hearing one man say.

''Lazy, nogoods,'' said another. ''You can't find a one who can work a full day.''

''I find if a man and his family are treated fairly, fed properly and given shelter, they will serve you well,'' Papa said.

''The Lord has blessed us with special people,'' Mama murmured, folding her napkin.

As for me, I could not imagine life without our special people. Especially Peter. Much as I loved my dear sister, she was still a sister, and a girl besides. No one could whistle louder than Peter. I could run faster, but he could beat me climbing any tree. When we all gathered for prayer meetings, Peter could say ''A-men'' for a full minute without taking a breath.

By the time Mama, Ann and I reached the bonfire near the old timbers, the singing had already started. Peter waved me over, and we jumped on a big fallen log. Everywhere we looked, we saw happy, smiling faces.

> *"The Lord's our Savior . . . "*
>   *(Clap, clap, clap)*
> *"He loves His children . . . "*
>   *(Clap, clap, clap)*
> *"He goin' take us with Him . . . "*
>   *(Clap, clap, clap)*

"Into joyful heaven . . . "
(*Clap, clap, clap*)

Strong voices filled the nighttime air with a chorus of crickets in the background. Somewhere in the distance an owl joined the song, his hooting a lonely and strange noise. Peter and I swung from side to side, clapping our hands.

When the song was over, Mama opened her Bible and read by the light of the fire. She told the story of Jesus, how He was born and grew up, how He helped people and gave His life because of His love for everyone. They were wonderful stories, and the people nodded and listened and asked to hear more.

Again we sang, our voices rolling across the lands of Terra Rubra. The moon covered the ground with a silver frost of light.

Finally, Mama motioned Ann and me over. As the gentleman, I stood between them as we returned to the house. We were just climbing the porch stairs when Mama turned to me.

"Frank, I wanted to tell Alfred I would be needing the good carriage in the morning. Mrs. Parker is sick and I have knitted her a shoulder shawl."

"All right, Mama, I'll go tell him," I offered.

I leaped down the steps, proud that my long legs could cover them two at a time. Alfred often slept all night in the blacksmith stable. I glanced over at the bonfire near the old timbers. Only a few golden logs remained, their embers dying fast.

Pounding on the stable door, I suddenly felt a chill. The night air had cooled. In a moment, Alfred appeared. He carried a flickering candle.

"Yes, Master Francis?"

"My mother will be needing the good carriage tomorrow, Alfred. She will be visiting Mrs. Parker in the morning."

"It will be ready for her, Master."

My message delivered, I headed back to the house. Once more I heard the owl hooting. It was a sad song, a plaintive call. I glanced toward the old timbers, wondering if the bird sat perched on one of the dead branches.

Without warning, I felt myself stumbling forward. Something was in my path—a big, unmoving object. I thrust my arms ahead, trying to break my fall, but I tasted the dust of Terra Rubra as I sprawled headfirst.

Slowly I sat up, rubbing the knee that had been first to feel the earth. I spit to the side in an effort to rid myself of the dirty taste in my mouth. Then I heard it—a low frightening moan.

As I strained to see in the moonlight, I could distinguish the form of a huge figure. I rubbed my eyes. Yes, it was a man. A giant of a man. A layer of glistening sweat covered his face—a face pitted with deep cuts and scars. I tried to get up, but my arms and legs would not move. I wanted to yell. Nothing would come out. Who was this strange man? I had never seen him before. I had never seen anything like him before.

Suddenly he moved forward. My heart pounded, and a quick cold dampness soaked into my clothes. In my head raced a thought I had heard my mother say many times: "The Lord is my helper, and I will not fear what man shall do unto me."

Again the man slid a few inches closer to me. Yes, yes, I knew the Lord was my helper—but I was filled with fear of this man before me.

Big Decisions

I held my breath. My mind kept telling me to run, but my body could not obey. Slowly I watched as the large figure before me rose to his feet. I closed my eyes, hoping that when I reopened them he would be gone. No, he was still there. His huge chest and shoulders blocked the moon from my sight.

"Uh-a-uh-imim—"

The sounds he uttered were strange to me. They were not words, only gurglings from his throat. Finally I managed to lift myself to my knees. I had gathered just enough strength and courage to make a run for it when the man staggered forward, knocked me backyards and pinned me to the ground. I squirm-ed, trying to free myself. It was easier than I expected. Suddenly, I knew why. The man was not trying to hold me. He had only collapsed on top of me. With a quick motion, I pulled myself completely away.

I started toward the house, then stopped. Glancing back, I saw the stranger was not moving. A thought hit me—maybe Alfred would know what to do. After all, this was a black man. Although he was not one of our slaves, Alfred seemed to know the black men and their families from all the nearby plantations.

Moments later, I stood in front of Alfred's door once again. He was slower in coming this time. Perhaps he had managed to get to sleep. How long had I been with the stranger? I could not answer. All I knew was that the clothes I wore felt moist and clammy.

Once I had poured my story out to Alfred, he told me to lead him to the man. As we walked, I had a fear that the stranger might have slipped away in the night. My fear was wasted. The man still lay where he had fallen. Alfred asked me to help carry the stranger back to the stablehouse. I lent what support I could, but in truth, it was Alfred who carried the fellow. Alfred, with his mighty arms and chest had been our blacksmith for as long as I could remember. His strength was ample proof of the power gained from pounding a mighty iron each day.

"Go now to your family," Alfred told me. "They shall miss you and worry. Say nothing about this."

I shook my head. "But do you know him? Why did he come here? Is he all right?"

Alfred turned to stare at the stranger. The candle cast a bright light on the man's face. It was clear he had been beaten, many times before and recently as well. Fresh open wounds blended with tired scars. Half of his shirt was ripped away, and there were ugly welts on his shoulders and back. The stranger breathed heavily, never once opening his eyes.

"I shall take care of him, Master Francis. Return to your family. By morning he may be better able to tell us something. Go, now."

I followed Alfred's order, knowing he spoke wisely. No candles burned in my sister's or my mother's rooms so I knew they had retired for the night. A sliver of light appeared at the bottom of the library door, but I thought it better not to bother Papa. He did not like to be interrupted while he was working.

By the time I slipped into a clean, dry nightshirt and found safety and warmth under my featherbed comforter, my heartbeat had returned to normal. Sleep did not come quickly. The face of the stranger lingered in my mind. I prayed for morning to come swiftly so I might learn more about him.

The first of the morning's sunrays awakened me. I washed and dressed swiftly, deciding to eat breakfast after I had returned from visiting Alfred. My stomach had no wish for food. I only wanted to find out about the stranger. But when I rushed downstairs, I heard voices in the kitchen. One of the voices was Alfred's. Another was Papa's. I wasted no time in getting there.

Alfred stood at one end of the kitchen table while the stranger stood beside him. At first, I thought only Papa was with them, but in a moment Mama entered through the pantry door.

Papa looked at me, stern eyes and wrinkles forming as he sipped a cup of tea. "You saw no cause to let me know of your discovery last night?" he asked.

I looked to Mama, but her eyes were lowered. "You were in the library, sir," I answered. "I thought it best not to disturb you. Mama had already gone to bed."

Papa nodded, satisfied with my answer. I sighed relief and moved to Mama's side.

"Well, Alfred, I am afraid your friend must return to his rightful master," Papa declared. "We can prepare a food pouch for him and then—"

"Begging the Master's pardon, sir, but it does not seem right to return him to a master who does nothing but beat and whip him. I spent the night cleaning his wounds. They have been made with chains and heavy rods." Alfred paused, his tongue wetting his lips.

"You are a fair master. Not all masters are like you. His must be a monster."

Papa took a long sip of tea. "I admit his wounds are sad indeed. I am sorry for what suffering this man must have endured."

"Then let him stay with us," Alfred suggested. "We will find a place for him. We will share our food."

Papa shook his head. "I am a judge, my friend. You are suggesting that I break the law. Someone has paid money for this man, therefore this man belongs to his master."

Without warning, Mama took a step forward. "John, we all belong to the same Master, God Almighty. This man is no different than any of us."

I could not believe my mother's words. Never had I heard her speak with such force—and to my father. Always she was quiet and supporting, seldom uttering the slightest word of disagreement. The expression on Papa's face told me he was equally surprised.

"The words you speak are true enough," Papa said, "but I must uphold the law. Would you suggest that I, a judge, harbor this fugitive? With what respect would people hold me? How could I live with myself?"

Mama moved to stand behind the stranger. "Could you live with yourself better knowing you would be sending this man back for more beatings and torture?"

I marveled at my mother. How strong she seemed. How forceful her words.

"There is still the law," Papa answered. "It is true enough this man has been mistreated. But would you have me break the law on his account?"

Mama stood firm. "There is the law of man and there is the law of God. Each of us must decide which is the greater law. But might I remind you of Romans 10:4 which says, 'Christ is the end of the law for righteousness to every one that believeth.' "

Silently, my father set his tea cup upon the table. He rubbed his chin, glancing first at Alfred and then at the stranger. Finally, Papa spoke once more.

"Perhaps it is well enough that we stand here discussing the future of this man, but he says nothing. Did he speak to you last night, Alfred?"

For a moment Alfred did not answer. Slowly he stood, pushed his chair back and walked to the stranger. He motioned my father forward to look into the man's face.

"Show the man why you do not speak, friend."

When the stranger opened his mouth, I gasped aloud. He had no tongue. Mama pulled me close to her, lowering her gaze to the floor.

"His master was not satisfied with beating him," said Alfred quietly. "He ordered his tongue ripped out too."

Papa did not speak for several minutes. In truth, there was not a sound in the entire kitchen. Finally, my father moved toward the pantry door.

"Can he write at all?" Papa asked Alfred.

"Only a few words. His name and that of his master."

Papa nodded. "Good. I shall want his master's name. I will write to his master and offer him a fair price for the man."

"What if his master refuses to sell?" Mama asked.

"I do not believe a plantation slavemaster who treats his slaves like this will want many questions asked," replied Papa. "I shall make my letter brief and to the point. By purchasing the slave fairly, we shall respect the law of man. By taking him in, I hope we are honoring the law of God."

As Alfred helped the stranger stand, I saw Papa glance at Mama. It was a kind look, a look of love and understanding. Mama moved to my father's side. "You are a good man," she said softly.

I could not have agreed more. Surely I had been blessed with a fine Father, I hoped the people who entered his courtroom knew this too—that John Key was a fair and honest man.

In the days and weeks that followed, I visited the stablehouse often. I learned that the stranger was known as Henry. He helped Alfred with the chores of blacksmithing. Slowly our new friend regained his strength. Finally, a letter arrived which sent me dashing to the stablehouse.

"You can stay with us, Henry!" I shouted. "My father is your master now. You can stay here at Terra Rubra!"

Henry's eyes said what his voice could not. They sparkled joyfully as he grabbed me up and swung me in wide circles around the stablehouse. Alfred laughed merrily.

" 'Tis a fine day for all of us!" Alfred declared. "Henry is a hard worker. He learns quickly too. The Lord be praised for this wonderful day!"

I visited the stablehouse often after that. Henry and I became close friends. When Papa told me I would be going to stay with Grandmother Key for awhile, I asked if Henry might drive me there in the carriage—with Peter too, of course.

Papa agreed.

Grandmother Key lived in a big, beautiful home called Belvoir. It was not far away from Chesapeake Bay and Annapolis, the capital city of Maryland. I knew I would miss Terra Rubra, but the sandy soils near Belvoir helped furnish fresh lobster, crab and oysters. For dessert, we often ate strawberries and juicy melons. All my clothes grew a bit snug when I stayed at Belvoir.

"I could eat this food forever!" I told Grandmother at supper one evening.

Grandmother smiled. "Young, growing boys *should* enjoy their meals. But remember, Francis, 'Man shall not live by bread alone, but by every word that proceedeth out of the mouth of God.' "

Yes, Grandmother Key was much like Mama. The Bible was their favorite companion. But sadly enough, Grandmother could not read the words she loved so dearly. Grandmother was blind. I had heard the story of how Grandmother became blind many times. She was a young girl, sleeping in her father's house, when she awoke to the sound of people yelling, "Fire!" The noise came from the slaves' quarters. Quickly Grandmother jumped from her bed and ran to the fire.

People were running around in confusion. The air was hot and filled with smoke. Suddenly a woman dashed forward.

"My children are still in the fire!" the woman cried. Other slaves surrounded the woman and stopped her from running into the flames.

No one noticed the small girl who was my grandmother. Quickly she raced into the burning house. She found the two children were huddled together in the back of one of the burning rooms. My grandmother grabbed their hands and pulled them forward. When they reached safety, they were hugged by everyone. Then my grandmother collapsed.

The next time she opened her eyes, my grandmother could not see. The smoke and the fire had stolen her sight.

Grandmother seldom spoke of her blindness. She knew every foot of Belvoir and had no trouble getting around her home. She was so kind and good that everyone loved to read to her. I treasured the times I was chosen. Sometimes I made up short stories and verses myself. Grandmother was my favorite audience.

"You have a way with words, Francis," she told me. "It is a gift from God. Now it falls upon you to make the most from that gift. Study hard, read whenever you can, and share kind words often."

Whenever I visited Grandmother, she invited Master Andrew Simmons to serve as my tutor. There were few schools in America; none near Terra Rubra. There was talk one would be opening soon in Annapolis.

"You are a fine scholar," the schoolmaster told me. "Your strength with words leads me to think you might make a fine lawyer some day . . . or perhaps a preacher for the Lord."

The schoolmaster's choices both sounded good to me. But for the present, I divided my time between the pleasures of Terra Rubra and Belvoir.

One morning I attended Sunday worship with my grandmother in Annapolis. We had barely arrived home after the service, when I glanced down the road and saw another carriage rolling up the dusty path. I cupped my hand to block out the morning sun. As the carriage neared, I recognized the driver. It was Henry. Quickly I raced to meet him on the road. His warm smile was a welcome sight. No sooner had I leaped and climbed my way to a spot beside him, when he handed me a letter. My father's seal enclosed its contents. I ripped the letter open and read my father's writing:

> *Young Master Key,*
>
> *Return to Terra Rubra as soon as possible. Most important visitor coming. Make haste.*
>
> *Your Loving Father*

For a moment I forgot Henry's sad problem and looked anxiously at him. "Who's coming?" I asked, not thinking that the poor man could give me no answer.

I scrambled down from the carriage and ran toward the house. I began packing at once. Father would not have sent Henry and the letter unless this visitor was important indeed! But who could it be? The question made my hands pack even faster.

Important Guest

"Oh, can't the horses go any faster, Henry? I can hardly wait to get back to Terra Rubra."

My heart pounded rapidly as our carriage rolled along the eighty miles that separated Annapolis from home. How I longed to jump on a horse and race homeward. I could hear my father's words to such a thought: "A boy of twelve has no business riding such a trail all alone. You are tall and sturdy, Francis, and you handle a horse with ease, but you would be no match for the thieves and villains that prowl the roads looking for victims."

I knew Father was right, of course. Visitors to Terra Rubra told stories of vicious attacks by robbing highwaymen. Henry and the carriage might be slower, but it was also safer. Soon Father would be giving me permission to make the ride by myself. For now, I was content to travel with the strong and powerful Henry by my side.

The closer we came to home, the more excited I grew. Ann was waiting on the front porch. I noticed strips of red, white and blue bunting wrapped around the railings. Suddenly I knew—I realized who our important guest must be!

"Isn't it wonderful, Francis! General George Washington himself coming to Terra Rubra!"

Ann's words confirmed my guess. Still it seemed too wonderful to believe. I dashed inside, looking for Father.

"Father! Father! Where are you?"

The house buzzed with activity. The house slaves were everywhere, dusting and cleaning. I spotted Peter at the top of the stairwell. He was carefully cleaning the carved wooden trim of the bannister. His face broke into a wide smile when he saw me.

"Master Francis, welcome back!"

"Thank you, Peter. Have you seen my father?"

"He was in the kitchen inspecting the venison."

Hurriedly I raced away. My father's face in the kitchen was a welcome sight indeed! The rich aroma of freshly-baked mincemeat pies mingled with the scrumptious smells of fresh bread.

"Is it really true, Father? Is General Washington truly coming to Terra Rubra?" I asked.

Father nodded. "It's true enough, Son. The General is traveling to the nation's capital in Philadelphia. He will be sharing a meal with us. I hope you will make us proud of you."

"I promise I will, Father. When will he arrive?"

"In a few hours." Father stopped a moment to sample a spoonful of venison dressing. He smiled at the cook, then handed the spoon back. "You'll have time for a good scrubbing, Francis. Mother has laid your clothes out on your bed."

Not wasting a moment, I ran upstairs. I had hoped Peter would still be there, but he was gone. The wooden stairwell gleamed in the sunlight.

Reaching my room, I found a bucket of water resting beside an empty basin with soap nearby.

Father had meant what he said about a good scrubbing. I washed my hands and face soundly, watching the water take on the reddish color of Terra Rubra.

Carefully I slipped into my clothes. Just as I was fastening the final button on my waistcoat, Ann appeared at the doorway.

"Mother sent me to help you with your sash," my sister said.

"What sash is that?"

Ann strolled to the dressing table and picked up a long ribbon. Actually, there were three ribbons stitched together. It was a bright red, white and blue.

"We are all wearing our country's colors," Ann explained, "in honor of General Washington's visit. Have you looked outside? The General's soldiers, men who fought with him in the struggle for independence from England, have come from miles away. They're wearing their war uniforms. We'll be giving the

General a fine welcome indeed. Now let us get you into your sash.''

Maybe it was our too eager fingers. Perhaps it was because we had never tied a sash like this one. Anyway, it took Ann and me five tries before we had the sash successfully draped across my shoulder and tied at the hip.

Suddenly, we heard the sound of men's voices in the distance. Ann and I raced to the window and gazed out. My sister had spoken the truth. Hundreds of soldiers dotted our front lawn and lined the path to the nearby town of Frederick.

''Look, there in the distance!'' Ann whispered. ''He's coming! He's really coming!''

Yes, I could see the movement of horses and people about a mile or so away. My heart pounded. General George Washington! President George Washington! He was coming to our house; to eat at our table.

''Oh, Francis, is my sash straight? And my dress—does it look all right?''

''You sound just like Mother, Ann.'' I teased. But I must confess that I did straighten my own sash a bit and smooth out my shirt. ''Come, Ann, let's go downstairs. We should be ready to greet Father on the porch.''

Both of us dashed to the door, raced down the staircase, across the entryway and outside. The cheers were louder as the cluster of horsemen approached. Men wore faded pants and coats—the old uniforms they had worn in the Revolution. Their families mingled freely, filling the entire front lawn.

There they came—his father and General Washington. The important guest rode a proud white horse. Was the horse's name Chestnut? I recall Father telling us about it once. Our servants rushed out to the men, taking their horses to a nearby hitching rack.

I felt my mother's hand slip onto my shoulder and I noticed the other hand rested on Ann's. I was glad she was there with us. I felt more secure, more at ease.

After General Washington had spent a long while greeting his old comrades, Father led him up the front steps. I could not help but notice the light layer of red dust that tinted the General's coat. No one escaped the markings of Terra Rubra.

"This is the mistress of my home," Father said, introducing my mother who gracefully curtsied to our guest. "And these are my two children, Francis Scott and Ann Charlton Key."

From the corner of my eye, I noticed Ann's attempted curtsy. It lacked the gracefulness of my mother's, but it was an admirable attempt. As for myself, I bowed low. Upon rising, I could tell from my father's smiling face that he was quite pleased with our efforts.

"I'll take our guest in the house to clean up a bit before dinner," Father said. "Frank, perhaps you'll see that the others are taken care of on the lawn."

"We will serve them outside," Mother offered. "We've plenty of ham and chicken for everyone."

"I knew we would be well treated at the home of John Key," General Washington laughed. "It sounds like a feast."

"It's not often we entertain such an honored guest," Mother replied.

I watched as the three of them entered the house. Then I turned and started down the steps.

"But what am I to do?" Ann asked, a woeful pout on her face.

"Come on, little one. Let's make sure our friends are well taken care of," I answered.

The front yard was crowded. People from miles around had come to see General Washington. Old soldier friends of Father were washing the dust of Terra Rubra from their faces. Our servants moved quickly, carrying washbasins filled with water and clean towels.

"Never seen anything like this!" Peter called to me. "We're all going to have a picnic outside here while you folks are eating inside."

"I wish you and everybody else could eat inside with us," I yelled back.

Peter smiled. "I like this better. I don't think I could eat a bite of food sitting in the same room as Master Washington. My, my! Did you see the way he sat on that horse of his? Never saw the like of that before!"

I nodded, only half listening to what Peter was saying. All I could think about was what he had said about eating. It suddenly occurred to me that I would not be able to eat either. I only hoped I would not make a fool of myself and reflect poorly on my father.

Ann grabbed my arm. Mother was standing on the porch waving us to come in. Quickly I followed my sister's lead.

Our dining room was filled with Father's soldier friends from nearby Frederick and General Washington's companions. When we were finally seated, I was just as happy I was not near our important guest. I would have surely spilled something.

The talk was loud and lively during dinner. Sometimes I strained to hear what my father and General Washington were saying, but they were too far away. I could tell many of the men were recalling their Revolutionary War days.

Finally, men began standing. I stood up and slipped to my father's side. General Washington looked at me and smiled.

"Maybe your son will take me to the upstairs portico?"

"A good thought!" Father said. "Frank, take our

guest upstairs. He's going to say a few words to our guests outside."

"I-I, well, certainly, Father."

It wasn't that I didn't want to take General Washington upstairs. It was just that being with him made me feel so clumsy. Sure enough, as we walked up the staircase, I stumbled. The General didn't say anything, but I could feel my face turning the color of Terra Rubra soil.

If that wasn't bad enough, I had to pull several times at the french doors at the end of the hall upstairs. Any other time, they opened easily. But not today! Not when I'm standing there with General Washington. That is when I have two fistfuls of thumbs.

As the general walked on to the portico balcony, a wild cheer went up from people below. I stepped back as my father came to introduce our guest. I felt proud listening to my father. His words came so freely, and I sensed that General Washington enjoyed the fine things my father said about him.

Next, it was time for General Washington. His words came freely too, his voice rolling clear and loud to all listening.

"My countrymen, I am about to leave your good land, your beautiful valleys, your refreshing streams, and the blue hills of Maryland which stretch before me. I cannot leave you, fellow citizens, without thanking you again and again for the true and devoted friendship you have shown me. In the darkest hours of our struggle for independence, of doubt and gloom, the help and support I received from the people of Frederick County always cheered me. It always woke a responsive echo in my heart. My heart is too full to say more. God bless you all."

God bless *you*, I thought to myself. As I listened

to the people cheering and watched their happy faces, I knew this was a day I would never forget. Never did I feel more proud to be an American. I felt grateful for having a family who loved me, a home that gave me happiness and joy, good friends and freedom. A light breeze danced across Terra Rubra. As I gazed upward, the clouds floated lazily along.

"Thank you, dear God," I whispered. "Thank you for everything."

Off to School

"You got the rest of your things packed, Master Francis?"

Peter stood in the doorway of my room. There was more than a trace of sadness in his voice. I nodded as I tied the final strap around the dressing case.

"This is the last," I answered. "I am grateful Father is allowing me to take the strongest pack horse for my things. An ordinary horse might not be able to make the trip to Annapolis with all I am taking. But Dusty is a good, strong animal."

Peter came forward and reached for the case. But I stepped in front of him and hugged him.

"I shall miss you, good friend. You and Terra Rubra and Ann and all the rest."

Peter backed away. "We will all be waiting for you when you come back, Master Francis."

For several moments after Peter left, I sat on my bed looking around the room. It was hard to leave. After so many years of having my father's study serve as a schoolroom, it would be strange to be among other boys at the new St. John's School in Annapolis. But

Uncle Philip lived in Annapolis. People spoke of him
as being among the finest lawyers in all of Maryland.
He always had a happy voice, laughing eyes and
cheerful manner. There was Grandmother Key in
nearby Belvoir. It was good knowing I could visit
there.

"Have you time for a poem?"

My sister Ann suddenly appeared at the doorway.
She held a fresh parchment.

"I suppose," I answered, a teasing note in my
voice. "But it had better be up to the Key quality."

Ann stood straight and proud. She looked like she
was ready to give a noteworthy address.

*"My brother goes off to school today
I shall miss him much I fear,
We have our feuds and battles
But I think him rather dear.*

*I'll miss our daily games, I know
At which I beat him fair,
I'll miss his merry smile and laugh
And I'll miss his curly hair!"*

I laughed loudly. "So, even today I must endure
my sister's teasing. Ah, well, it is just as well. 'Be
thyself, at all times,' Mother says. 'Be true and
honest.' I can tell the world that my sister Ann is one
big tease."

"Oh, Frankie, how I'm going to miss you!" Ann
ran to me, throwing her arms around my shoulders.

"I'm not going off forever," I reminded her.
"You're not rid of me that easily."

Ann pulled away and shook her head. "I promised myself I wouldn't cry and now look what you've
done—you made me cry. You should be ashamed!"
Pretending to be disgusted, Ann bounced out of my
room. If she had remained much longer, I might have
found myself in tears too.

I was glad Father was riding with me. I felt older and more independent going to school in Annapolis, but I did not feel ready to be left completely on my own.

The first night of our journey, we stayed overnight in Taneytown. The owner of the inn treated us well, taking good care of our horses and feeding us a delicious meal. I knew it was because of Father. Everyone respected Squire Key of Terra Rubra. It was a good feeling being his son.

Grandmother Key entertained us on the second night of our travels. The candles burned long into the night as we visited. We left early the next morning, hoping to take care of my enrollment at St. John's and to visit Uncle Philip as well.

I must confess that St. John's Preparatory School and College left me with a sick feeling when I first saw it. Having come from the mighty brick and wood of our home at Terra Rubra to the big, dark walls of St. John's left me homesick.

"Remember what your mother tells us," suggested Father. "You can judge little on what the eyes can see. It is what lies beneath the surface that is more important."

"But Mother says that of people," I answered. "There seems to be little life to St. John's."

"Make such judgments slowly," Father replied.

In fairness, the headmaster at St. John's was friendly enough. I did not like the way he constantly tugged at his reddish moustach, but I had to admit the color reminded me of Terra Rubra. Father gave him money for my enrollment and we left. Classes would begin early the next morning. I was eager for the fun of being with Uncle Philip.

The evening with Uncle Philip was all I had hoped for—and more. I ate enough ham to last me for a month! But I still found room for two pieces of spice cake. I should not say pieces, for they were more like the mountains and hills of Terra Rubra.

"Growing boys must eat," my uncle laughed when my father cautioned about the amount of my consumption.

My father shook his head. "He is eating like he will never eat another meal!"

"Young Frankie will need his strength," said Uncle Philip. "His Great-aunt Scott counts her pennies carefully. She is known to set a thin table some evenings. And the boys of St. John's—well, a newcomer must win his place among them. Let the boy eat, John. Let the boy eat."

I soon discovered that Uncle Philip spoke the truth.

My Great-aunt Scott, with whom I was to board while I attended St. John's, believed the greatest sin in the world was waste. Money, time, food, clothing—each had its own use and no small particle was to be squandered. Words, too, had their purpose and she found no purpose at all in idle chatter or gossip. But she was a giving person, generous and kind.

"Throw those bread crumbs to the birds," she told the house servants who attended us at dinner. "And heat some water for those meat bones. It will make for good strong broth."

After such pronouncements, my Great-aunt always smiled, seemingly proud with such decisions. I felt safe in her care—a safety I did not feel at school.

What makes some people dislike another without reason? Maybe it was because I had not lived in Annapolis all my life. Perhaps some of the boys did not like the way I spoke . . . or walked . . . or laughed. I really do not know. One thing was certain. From the first day at St. John's, I was teased about my hair.

"Curly Key!" one boy shouted. A few other boys picked up the chant. "Curly Key! Curly Key!" I

remembered Ann's gentle teasing, but this was not
the same.

At first, I tried to ignore the yells. ''Turn the other
cheek,'' I recall my mother saying. ''Remember how
the good Lord endured name calling and beatings.
He is our example. Lift not a hand in anger against
your enemies. Treat them with kindness.''

Over and over I repeated her words. Night after
night I prayed for strength to ignore the jeers and
chants . . . but they got worse.

"Master Key, with locks so curly
Is he a boy or is he a gir-lie?"

I gritted my teeth. I clenched my fists. I tried to
push the sound of their voices out of my head. I longed
for a chance to talk with my father. Great-aunt Scott
would not understand. She was always saying good
things about my hair. She did not know the suffering
it brought to me.

By the end of the first week, I knew I could not take the teasing much longer. I decided to visit Uncle Philip.

"So the boys don't like your curls, eh, Frankie? Well, the important thing is how *you* feel about them."

Uncle Philip leaned back in his chair. He studied me carefully.

"I don't know. I've always wanted to have my hair cut short," I said. "But I would never want to hurt Mother or Father. They like my hair long."

Uncle Philip leaned forward. "But they are not here, boy. And your hair is *your* hair. If a haircut would ease your suffering, then a haircut you should have. By the time your parents see you again, it will have grown back."

It sounded like a wise solution. Father had always told me to solve my own problems. This way I would not have to trouble my parents at all. They would not be hurt by what they did not know . . . or see.

"Do you know anyone who would cut my hair?" I asked.

Uncle Philip stood up. "We shall have it done this very afternoon. Meet a problem head on, I say. Take care of it at once."

At dinner that evening Great-aunt Scott said little about the curls which had disappeared. But I caught her stare several times. Finally, I knew I must say something.

"I-I hope you do not mind my new appearance," I mumbled. "It was just that I was weary of my curls."

My Great-aunt set her spoon beside the bowl of soup she had been sipping. She looked at me sternly.

"And the boys of St. John's had nothing to do with it?"

My mouth opened in surprise. How did she know?

"Well, I-I must confess they did not take kindly to my curls. But how did you know?"

"Your father suffered much the same abuse when he was a boy your age. Your Uncle Philip, as well. I am not surprised that you took the action you did. I only regret that you did not come to me with your problem."

"But you're so old—"

The moment the words left my mouth I wished for them back. How could I be so unkind, such a fool, I had not meant to say that.

Great-aunt Scott simply shook her head. A smile curled her lips.

"Francis, you must remember that I was young once. Strange as it seems, I can even recall the hurts I felt as a child. Now and then I came to the dinner table wearing a sad face. I was a tall child, and I was teased unmercifully."

I squirmed on my chair. I sensed it was not pleasant for my Great-aunt to relive her past in this conversation.

"But soon my friends grew taller and I stopped. The teasing stopped. And I realized much of my suffering was of my own making. Always be willing to accept criticism, young Francis, but do not let lesser people make you unhappy."

For the first time, I saw my Great-aunt Scott in a different way. Although she was much older than I, she understood. Just as Uncle Philip had understood, she did too. How foolish I had been. If only young people realized how helpful and wise older people could be.

Without my curls, I felt happier returning to St. John's. I decided to be ready for any other teasing I would receive. One boy pointed at me and yelled, "Curly Key's been scalped!" I pretended not to hear and walked on.

Another boy asked me, "Where's your curls, Master Key?"

"Well, I needed a softer pillow," I answered, "so I snipped them off and put them in a cotton bag."

No longer did the remarks bother me. When anyone said something about my curls—or the lack of them, I merely said something back. The boys seemed to like my answers.

"You have a sharp wit about you, Frank," one boy said.

"Always quick with the answers," added another.

Two of my schoolmates, Daniel Murray and John Shaw, became my companions. We studied together during the week. On warm days, we went swimming and riding. When the lake near St. John's froze over, we went skating. Even when we had nothing to do, we did it together. It felt good to have friends.

As the day approached for final exams at the end of the first term, everyone began studying. Students who did not score well would not be allowed to return to St. John's. I spent every spare minute with my nose in books.

But once the tests were over and we were sure we passed, Daniel, John and I went looking for fun. We found it at Uncle Philip's. A large steer stood tied to the hitching post in front of his office.

"The farmer had no money to pay me," Uncle Philip explained. "He left me with his steer, Edward. I hope to sell him to another client who is coming tomorrow."

"May we borrow him this afternoon?" I asked. "I'll bring him back."

Uncle Philip rubbed his chin. "Just what would you do with a steer?"

"I'll tell you later, Uncle. Please trust me."

An hour later Daniel, John and I led Edward into

the courtyard of St. John's. Quickly boys clustered around us.

"Where did you get this animal?" a classmate asked.

My eyes twinkled with mischief. "He's a prize. The headmaster gave him to me for scoring the highest grades on my exams."

A trickle of laughter mushroomed into a loud roar. Although I was doing well in my classes, I was not the class leader in any one of them and my classmates knew it.

"Anyone want a ride?" I shouted.

No one volunteered. Edward *looked* tame enough, but not a soul was willing to test the animal.

"Why don't you ride him, Key?" a voice called out.

"Yes, you show us how."

Soon all were shouting for me to climb aboard the steer. Only for a moment did I hesitate. I moved the crowd back so I could get a run behind the steer. Once on Edward's back, I discovered the animal was not as quiet and peaceful as I thought. He pawed the ground and shook his head. Suddenly, he became bounding and alive. I grabbed his neck as he began dashing around the courtyard. He stopped without warning, then leaped ahead. He turned and jumped.

"Hold on, Key!" John shouted.

"You can do it!" Daniel yelled.

Do it I did, for ten seconds more. Then, with a quick burst of speed and a sudden stop, Edward showed his greatest skill at ridding himself of unwanted cargo. I felt myself spinning into the air and landing on the hard ground. I sat for a minute, confused and dazed. The sounds of the other boys reminded me of where I was.

"You can really ride, Key!"

"I never thought you could do it, Curly. I mean, Frank."

In truth, I wasn't sure I could do it myself. But one thing was certain. My life changed that day. St. John's no longer was a place I dreaded. I began to enjoy my classes and classmates more. They liked me too.

When I returned to Terra Rubra, Mother and Father noticed the change in me.

"You're becoming a young man, Francis," Father told me. "The boy is growing up."

Mother was pleased, but displayed her usual cautious attitude. "Develop confidence in your talents, son, but beware of vanity. Remember the words of Proverbs 16:18 'Pride goeth before destruction, and a haughty spirit before a fall.' Turn to your schoolmaster for knowledge, but look to the Bible for direction and faith."

I hugged them both tightly. I knew the Lord had blessed me with wonderful parents. I hoped I would make them proud of me.

Poems for Polly

"Is war ever really necessary?"

Having posed his question, the schoolmaster look-
ed around the classroom. I sank lower into my chair.
I had no answer for the question. I was glad to see
Daniel's hand in the air.

"Yes, Mr. Murray?"

"We had no choice in our fight against England,"
Daniel said. "They wanted to control us. We tried
to reason with King George but he would not listen."

The schoolmaster scratched his head. You could
never tell whether an answer completely satisfied him.
He always wanted us to think more, to discover other
ways of reasoning.

"Any other comments? Master Key, you usually
have a few thoughts for us to ponder."

I sat up in my chair. "I'm afraid the topic is difficult for me."

Perhaps, just perhaps, the schoolmaster might let
me by today. It was a wasted thought.

"Difficult topics are those most worthy of discussion, Master Key. Please, share with us."

"Well, I doubt if war is ever really necessary," I replied. "But it is unavoidable sometimes. The Lord has given men minds to use. If used properly, war should be avoidable."

The schoolmaster eased to the window, obviously considering my thoughts. Slowly he turned. "You have brought the Lord into our discussion, Master Key, and I cannot raise any objection to that. War is a moral issue. But do I not recall my Bible correctly when I quote Exodus 15:3 which reads, 'The Lord is a man of war.'? It would thus seem our Supreme Being supports war."

So, it was to be this kind of discussion. I admired our schoolmaster. He stretched our minds and made us develop our own thoughts. And with my admiration for him, I blessed my mother and grandmother. How grateful I felt for their use of the Bible with me.

"You quote Exodus correctly," I answered. "But the Lord wages war against the Devil and sin. He reaches out to us and asks us to join Him in His fight. Better we look to the Book of John 4:8. It is there stated, 'God is love.' If we accept these words and follow the example of living given us by the Lord, then we will not feel that war is necessary."

The time for class to end arrived. I was grateful. As I left the room, the schoolmaster stopped me.

"You have a good mind, Master Key. You are young and innocent in the ways of the world. But your ideas have value." The schoolmaster paused. "What do you see for your future?"

I shook my head. "I have made no decisions, sir. Sometimes I think I would like to be a lawyer like my Uncle Philip."

"A good man," the schoolmaster observed. "Both your father and your uncle have made fine contributions to justice in Maryland."

"Thank you. But at times, I lean toward becoming a preacher."

"You have a quick remembrance and understanding of the messages of the Good Book. Today was not the first time you have shown this."

"I know I will have to make a decision soon," I replied.

"Indeed. But I have little fear you will make a wise one. Perhaps a bit wiser than riding a wild steer."

The schoolmaster's words amazed me! He knew about Edward. I sensed my face grow warm and flushed. My gaze dropped down, but the schoolmaster lifted my chin with his hand.

"A youth *should* have spirit and adventure," he said. "But I believe it is Proverbs that reminds us that 'The wise shall inherit glory.' Be sure you are willing to apply your heart too."

I nodded. "I shall."

Time drifted swiftly by at St. John's. My grades improved steadily. History and Latin became my favorite courses. Uncle Philip told me often that this meant I was destined to become a lawyer.

"And a virtuous one at that!" he declared. "I can envision you in the courtroom—in one hand a law book and in the other, the Bible. It is a worthy combination, my young nephew."

I must confess that when I was not studying my school books, I found myself in Uncle Philip's law library. I was fascinated with the Constitution of the United States. Whenever I could, I visited the gallery of the Maryland Legislature and listened to the representatives discuss issues.

And then, on a bright and brisk morning in June of 1796, my life at St. John's came to an end. Graduation. I joined the eighteen other men in my class as we received our diplomas. It was not easy saying goodbye.

"Well, if you ever need a good physician, you can come and knock on my door," John Shaw laughed. "Of course, I'll be charging you fellows double the usual rates for my services."

"And why might that be?" I asked.

"For all your foolish pranks and troubles you put me in," he answered. "Had it not been for you two, Master Francis Key and Master Daniel Murray, I'd probably have received the top honors in our class."

The three of us roared with laughter. But in truth, there was much to what John said.

"And what do you plan to do now?" I asked Daniel.

My friend shook his head. "I'm not certain. I've been told I have a good head for figures so perhaps I'll look for a position as a clerk. What about you, Frank?"

The decision had not come easily. Many nights I had stayed awake thinking about my future. I had prayed for the Lord's direction. Now, at the age of seventeen, I made my announcement.

"I'm going to become a lawyer," I said, mustering as much firmness as I could. "I guess it's in the family blood."

"Well," John proclaimed, "if I become a physician and you a lawyer, we shall hire Dan to be our clerk and gather our money."

"And he'll jump upon the fastest horse and run off with it!" I laughed, giving my friends hearty slaps on the back. They joined my laughter, then sadly we parted.

It was good to return to Terra Rubra. It always stayed the same. I loved riding up the flattened path to the long front porch, then circling around behind the house where the two wings of the house fanned outward. It was like being welcomed by giant arms.

Though time had little changed Terra Rubra, it had

touched the lives of those I loved. Ann was no longer my dirty-faced playmate. She was a young lady whose eyes sparkled like morning dew and whose figure neatly graced fine full frocks. Peter had gone off to find his family "somewhere in North Carolina."

"It is not quite the same," I told my mother.

She nodded. "Nothing ever stays the same, Francis. Look at you. Tall, slender, a fine cut of a fellow, if I do say so myself."

The words were welcome. I sensed my mother's pride, and I hoped to always be worthy of it.

I had not been home long when a letter arrived from Uncle Philip. He had promised to find another lawyer who might allow me to study law with him.

"I'll not take you myself, Frank," my uncle had laughed. "We are too much alike. I'd be likely to spoil you. But I'll find you a good teacher, you mark my words."

Uncle Philip was true to his promise.

Judge Jeremiah Chase was one of the most respected lawyers in Annapolis. Known to all for his honesty, he enjoyed a thriving practice. Each year he took only a few young men on as students in his office. When Uncle Philip told me that the judge had accepted me, I was delighted.

"You must have offered him all of Terra Rubra in exchange for working with me!" I exclaimed.

"Oh, not all of it," Uncle Philip laughed. "I made him promise to let you sleep in the pig pens when you go home. He agreed."

I soon discovered Judge Chase to be a demanding teacher indeed. Hour after hour, I poured over his law books, studying case after case. Words, words, words. They fascinated me, challenged me, frustrated me, thrilled me. I had always tossed words around so recklessly, enjoying their use in cheerful poems and letters.

In Annapolis there is a clerk
Every moment is spent at work,
Such a life is only strife
I much prefer a laughing wife!

Light, simple merriment had been my use of language. But as I read law book upon law book, I found the serious side of words. Careful and exact. No misunderstandings. Each night, I shared my readings and thoughts with Judge Chase. He took the law seriously, as almost a sacred faith. Our conversations were filled with questions and discussions, the judge always pushing me to think more deeply.

"Law exists for man to live a life that is safe, secure and just," the judge emphasized often, a thin, shaking finger raised to add force to his words. "To become a lawyer is to assume an honored trust."

I came to know the other five students who were studying with Judge Chase. I especially enjoyed the company of Roger Brooke Taney. A tall fellow, his head was crowned with the same kind of curly hair that rested on mine.

"Were you ever called 'Curly'?" I asked him one day.

He nodded. " 'Curley Taney' was a label I heard far too often," he admitted. "And a few of the fellows who shouted it ended up on the ground, I might mention."

"I was 'Curly Key' as a boy," I said. "My sister teased me without mercy. I heard it more than once at St. John's too."

"Well, let us make our own law," Roger declared. "I am forbidden to call you 'Curly Key' and you are forbidden to address me as 'Curly Taney.' "

"A fair arrangement," I laughed. "But we had better keep our law from the judge. He should not like us enjoying such humor."

Taney became a close companion. When I went to Terra Rubra for visits, he came with me often. He took a quick fancy to Ann and I sensed she returned his attentions eagerly. When I asked what she most enjoyed about him, the mischievous mask of childhood returned to her face.

"Why, his hair, of course!" she laughed. "His is darker than yours, my dear brother, but it twirls and curls just the same."

Ann, Ann, forever the tease. I prayed that time would never steal the joy and beauty of girlish spirit from her.

And while Ann provided a special delight for me at Terra Rubra, another young lady brought new life to Uncle Philip's home in Annapolis. He surprised the family with the announcement that he was marrying none other than the governor's daughter, a young woman known to all for her beauty and charm. Their marriage welcomed a new life style to our chambers in Annapolis. Guests came and went often. Evening and dinner parties were numerous. With my study of law, I combined a mastering of the latest dances. I must confess the sights and sounds of young ladies was a welcome change from the serious and stern Judge Chase.

Not that I ignored my studies. Taney would not have allowed that. He was caught up in the law completely. Only when we traveled to Terra Rubra did he shed the skin of scholarship. I enjoyed the social life of my uncle's home. Each party brought new faces and life into my world. One new face brought a special delight. Her name was Mary Tayloe Lloyd.

I am not sure what really attracted me to Mary Tayloe Lloyd. It could have been her deep dark eyes. Perhaps it was her fine pure skin. The first time I met her I sensed she was proud. She carried herself like a queen, her tall lithe frame gracefully dancing at parties, sitting poised and straight as she sipped tea or nibbled daintily at a cookie. Whatever it was, I felt drawn to her.

"Do you like poetry?" I asked her one night at one of Uncle Philip's parties.

Mary's eyes sparkled. "I like poetry well enough," she answered. "Do you?"

"Indeed I do!" I replied. "I have written verse for years. Some people think I have a talent for poems."

Mary was not impressed. "I shouldn't know about such things."

"Perhaps I might write you a poem or two."

"Suit yourself," Mary said. "I shall read them if I have time."

Yes, Mary Tayloe Lloyd was proud, perhaps arrogant and vain. But she fascinated me nonetheless. I set out to win her heart. I decided words would be my weapons.

> *So like a lady with smile so sweet*
> *So like a queen from head to feet,*
> *Always so pleasant, never annoyed*
> *So grand a person is Mary Lloyd.*

I loved writing such poems. It did not disturb me when I learned Mary was only fourteen. What difference do years make? Some people are young and merry at the age of ninety. Grandmother Key was like that. So, too, did Great-aunt Scott live with youthful spirit. Yet one of our fellows studying with Judge Chase was only twenty years of age but acted as if he were eighty. Mary was truly a young lady, far beyond her mere fourteen years. I began calling her Polly, only because I wanted to enjoy a special place with her.

"Polly, indeed!" Mary laughed. "Frank, you always have a new surprise for me."

"I hope you find favor in my surprises," I said.

And so I continued my offerings. In time, I came to a point where I felt I should declare my true feelings.

> *My love for you is ever growing*
> *Like a long river, ever flowing,*
> *To say your name is to sing a song*
> *When we're apart, the hours are long.*

At first, Polly laughed at my attempts to gain her attention. "I curl my hair with the notes you send me," she teased. "The paper is perfect for curling hair." But slowly I noticed she looked forward to my messages.

I soon realized that my goal of becoming a lawyer was not the only direction my life was taking. I also hoped to make Mary Tayloe Lloyd my wife. I prayed that I was not being too greedy.

Into the Courtroom

"You are making the candlemaker a wealthy man!"

Taney's voice startled me as I poured over a collection of papers on my study table. But I was grateful to see my friend. It gave me a good excuse to rise and stretch.

"Ah, I have two briefs to present before our distinguished judge and teacher tomorrow," I answered. "You know how he is when we're not prepared."

Taney nodded. "All too well."

I smiled at Taney. He was willing to sympathize with me, but in truth, he was always prepared. His presentations before the judge were organized and detailed. His answers were always right on the mark.

"It won't be long before we'll be taking our final tests," my friend said, collapsing on my bed. "Have you made any plans for the future?"

"I'm hopeful Uncle Philip will take me into his practice," I replied. "He is always saying he has more clients than he needs."

"Have you spoken to him about it?"

"No, but I think it's understood."

Taney stared at the ceiling. "I only wish I had an Uncle Philip. My future is a bit more foggy."

I looked at my friend. How I admired his fine mind, his happy wit and clever humor. Someday I knew Taney would be a lawyer of quality and virtue. But now he could find little direction to his life. I was grateful for my faith. I recalled the verse from Proverbs that said "In all thy ways acknowledge Him, and He shall direct thy paths." Whatever problems I had, I knew the Lord was always listening. The problems I faced in life were His tests of my faith. It gave me strength to know He was with me. It was a strength I would need in the days ahead.

One night after Uncle Philip and I had retired to his study, he asked me to sit down. I sensed something was wrong.

"Frank, I'm going to be closing up my law practice here in Annapolis," he said, lighting his pipe. "The wife and I are going to move to Washington."

I could not believe my ears. Everything I had heard about life in the new Capital was terrible. Half completed buildings, roads full of holes, thriving flies and rats—

"I can tell you're surprised," Uncle Philip continued. "Well, it's just that I've done about all I can here. I like to think I've got a little bit of pioneering blood in me. Washington's just getting started. I fancy they'll be needing a good lawyer or two. You finish up your studies, get a little experience and come and join me. I hope by then I'll be settled in and need some help."

It was too much for me to think about all at once. I thanked my uncle for sharing his plans with me and went to my bedroom.

Sleep did not come easily that night. "My future

is a bit more foggy,'' Taney had said. Now mine was foggy as well. My head was filled with unanswered questions. Would I pass the tests that would admit me to the Maryland Bar? I had been told the exams were not easy. If I failed, what would I do? What of Polly? Did she care anything for me, as I cared for her? Perhaps I was only fooling myself into thinking she might be a part of my future.

"In all thy ways acknowledge Him, and He shall direct thy paths.'' The words I had spoken to Taney returned to me. Have faith. Pray. Live life the best way possible. What more could I do?

I directed all my attention to my studies. When the exams came, I was fully prepared. Both Taney and I passed easily. We were attorneys!

Happily I returned to Terra Rubra. Good news was waiting.

"My cousin Arthur wants you to know you are welcome to apprentice with his law firm in Frederick,'' Mother announced. "Perhaps you could do that while your Uncle Philip is getting established in Washington.''

It was a wonderful offer. I had always liked Arthur. I would gain experience and be able to live at Terra Rubra. But what of Polly? I shared my concern with my sister Ann.

"If she cares about you, she will wait,'' Ann said with a nod. "In truth, I must confess you have become quite a handsome and respectable gentleman, my curly-haired brother.''

"The most handsome and respectable young attorney you know?'' I teased, knowing my sister had completely lost her heart to my friend Roger Taney.

"Perhaps the second best!'' she laughed.

In the months that followed, I devoted myself to working in Frederick. Cousin Arthur was patient with me, carefully explaining each case to which he assign-

ed me. Mostly I handled land survey questions and
wills. But now and then, I was allowed to take cases
into the courtroom. I enjoyed speaking before a judge
and watched his every move.

"I should like to have you as a lawyer, Master
Key," one judge told me after a case was over. "You
handle facts as a blacksmith pounds a shoe, with force
and fury. You are most convincing."

Such praise was welcome.

And welcome too were the trips I made to Annapolis. I kept the post busy with letters to Polly, but
nothing could take the place of actually being with
her. With each visit, I sensed we had become closer.
Only sixteen, she seemed more like a young woman
of twenty. Her cheerful spirit, her spritely manner,
her loveliness—all delighted me.

"Sometimes . . . sometimes I dream about you
. . . about you being my wife," I finally blurted out
one night as we walked in her backyard.

"How foolish!" she answered.

"Yes, I know."

"Francis Scott Key!" Polly stopped, took my arm
and faced me directly. "What I mean to say is that
it is foolish to dream about things that can happen.
Dreams should be saved for things that are impossi-
ble . . . or can only happen in the far future."

I was dumbfounded.

"What are you saying Polly?"

"I am saying that instead of merely dreaming of
me being your wife, why don't you ask me?"

Surely she was teasing. So often she led me along
with silly stories and riddles. But I pressed onward.

"All right, playful Polly, what would you say if I
asked you to marry me?"

Shaking her head, the lovely lass before me faked
a deep curtsey.

"Why, Master Key, you would have to ask my

father, of course. As for me, I shall not be married until I am seventeen which would mean waiting one year. But if the Colonel agrees to your request, and you are willing to wait, I shall be pleased and honored to become your loving wife.''

Polly, oh, Polly, I thank you.

Glory to you, oh Lord.

Quietly I pulled the young woman who would be my wife close to me. It was a moment I would never forget.

Word Wizard

January, 1802.

Annapolis shivered in cold winter breezes. Snow crusted the land, the narrow streets and alleys.

But freezing temperatures could not cool the warmth of love that filled my life. Polly. Divine Polly. I could think of little else.

On a cold winter morning, carriage after carriage rolled up to the Lloyd mansion in Annapolis. From Baltimore and Washington, the people came. They came from Frederick too. I met cousins I had never known. Uncles, aunts. All bringing wishes of joy and happiness.

"I've never seen so many people," Taney laughed. "All of them come to see a beautiful, golden-haired princess marry a shiftless, curly-headed attorney. It's hard to believe."

I laughed. "How good it is to have friends like you. Well, let us get on with this business."

The Lloyd home sparkled. For weeks the servants had polished, cleaned and shined every inch of the beautiful mansion. Candles glowed from every holder, matching the merry glow on the faces of the guests.

But as bright and as sparkling as the Lloyd home was, it could not match the beauty of my beloved Polly. Lace and satin swirled around her. She was a royal flower, a blossom in regal bloom.

And as we exchanged our pledge of love in marriage, I thanked God for giving me this wonderful girl. When the minister closed the service with the words, "What therefore God hath joined together, let not man put asunder," I declared a loud "Amen."

It was with little joy I brought Polly back to a small brick house I had rented for us in Frederick. It seemed like such a shack, a tiny dismal hut.

"I would buy you a castle if I could," I told her.

My new bride laughed. "It's a lovely house, Francis Scott Key, and I'll not have you belittle it. It's ours to live in and enjoy. Now enough of your silliness."

I had worried about bringing Polly to Frederick. Having grown up in Annapolis, she was accustomed to grand parties and a fancy life. Frederick was so much smaller with a quieter style of living. I feared Polly would find life dull.

But she surprised me. Neighbors quickly became our friends. She took up quilting, joining other womenfolk for afternoons of sewing. We entertained guests for supper and were invited out often.

There was no time to waste at Cousin Arthur's law offices. New businesses arrived daily to Frederick. Glassworks, grist mills, iron furnaces, furniture factories and paper mills grew larger. In 1803, President Jefferson bought a new piece of land called the Louisiana Purchase. Stagecoaches and Conestoga wagons rolled into town every day. Some of the travelers stayed. Cousin Arthur and I were kept busy every moment. When Taney wrote me of the problems he was having in Annapolis, I replied at once.

"Come to Frederick," I wrote. "There is plenty

of room for another lawyer. Anyway, it would bring you closer to a certain sister of mine who does nothing but talk about you.''

Taney took my suggestion. Whether or not it was the prospect of more business or the hope of seeing Ann, I do not know. But within weeks, we were hanging out his shingle that welcomed clients. Not long afterward, Terra Rubra witnessed a truly grand spectacle when my sister Ann became Mrs. Roger Brooke Taney.

Although Polly and I had come to enjoy life in Frederick, we welcomed Uncle Philip's invitation to come to Washington. He had found us a home in nearby Georgetown, right beside the Potomac River. It was a narrow house, but it contained a drawing room, sitting room, kitchen, dining room, conservatory, two large bedrooms on the second floor and four tiny bedrooms in the attic.

''It is a lot of house for just the two of us,'' I told Polly.

Her eyes danced. ''There may not always be two of us,'' she laughed.

True to her word, Polly soon made me a proud father. We had our new daughter christened Elizabeth Phoebe.

With the birth of Elizabeth came a new awareness of how the Lord had blessed me. A loving wife in Georgetown, my wonderful family at Terra Rubra, meaningful work with Uncle Philip in Washington—I felt ashamed at having complained about the dusty and torn roads on the way to work and the carelessness I found shown by some judges in the courtroom. Why are people so blind to the gifts God bestows? Why do we moan about small displeasures when we are surrounded by those we love and enjoy good health? I pledged to become a more useful servant to the Lord. I promised to be a loving husband and father. I offered my services as a member of the parish council at St. John's Episcopalian Church in Georgetown.

The summers always found us back at Terra Rubra. Polly grew to love the Key home plantation as much as I did. Rooms that had once been closed off were reopened as we were blessed with more children. Maria Lloyd joined Elizabeth, and then we welcomed Francis Scott, Jr.

Uncle Philip made many new friends in Washington. Soon there was talk about him running for Congress. I had given little thought to politics myself, although my respect for the President was great indeed. I had the clerk in our law office use his finest handscript in creating a wall hanging which read:

> *The God who gave us life, gave us*
> *liberty at the same time.*
>   *Thomas Jefferson*

It was a worthy thought.

I was also impressed with a lighter sentiment the President expressed. He was asked how he managed to remain calm in the face of many problems and responsibilities.

"When angry, count ten before you speak." he answered. "If very angry, count to one hundred."

I passed the President's suggestion on to Polly.

"You remember it as well!" she laughed. "I have seen your face redden whenever you are disturbed while at work. We shall all learn from President Jeffferson's fine words."

"Fair enough," I agreed.

When Uncle Philip did make his step and run for Congress, I inherited the entire law practice. It seemed foolish to travel from Georgetown to Washington each day. Anyway, I wanted to be near the children in their early growing years. Polly and I simply moved the law office into our home.

It was an unusual collection of people who made their way to my law offices. Uncle Philip referred many of his rich and powerful friends to me. Negro slaves, trying to win their freedom, came to ask for my help. Soldiers who had fought with Father in the War of Independence sought my help. I was happy to assist them without charge. Surely they had already paid enough by winning our country's freedom.

"You shall never be a rich man," Polly teased.

I smiled. "Perhaps not in money, my love. But it is a joy to serve others, especially those who need help the most."

I was soon to find two men who needed help desperately. Their names were Erich Bollman and Samuel Swartout. It was a case that placed me in direct opposition to the President of the United States.

A man named Aaron Burr had served as vice-president to Jefferson during his first term of office. Burr was an ambitious man. In truth, he had originally won the presidency as much as Jefferson. Burr and Jefferson had won an equal number of electoral votes. But when the election then went to the House of Representatives, Jefferson won out. A good friend of Taney's, Alexander Hamilton, spoke forcefully for Jefferson and persuaded many congressmen to vote for him. Jefferson was elected.

Bitter and angry, Burr later challenged Hamilton to a duel and killed him. Hamilton had been popular in Washington. Burr had few friends.

Now it was said Burr was trying to start his own country. He was arrested for taking weapons and men to the southwest. He asked Henry Clay to defend him against the treason charges.

Erich Bollman and Samuel Swartout were Burr's messengers. They were caught carrying secret plans. I was asked to defend them.

"It's a sticky business," Uncle Philip told me as

we ate supper one evening. "Burr is a dangerous man, capable of any evil deed. These men of his, Bollman and Swartout, are no better. They ought to toss the lot of them into the sea."

"Is that what President Jefferson says?" Polly asked, pouring our teacups to the brim.

"Indeed!" Uncle Philip answered.

I wondered whether or not I should tell my uncle the news. Perhaps it might be better to let the good meal within us settle in comfort and enjoy pleasant conversation.

"I have been asked to defend Bollman and Swartout." The words tumbled out of my mouth without effort. I watched Uncle Philip as his eyes widened and his mouth opened in surprise.

"You're-you're not going to do it, I trust?" he said.

I nodded. "Yes, I think I am."

"But Frank, you know how the President feels about this whole thing. We're talking about treason! You have established such a fine reputation in the courtroom. Just yesterday, I heard people talking about the brilliant way you handled the impeachment case against old Judge Chase. But this is treason—"

"Is an accused traitor or traitors not entitled to a fair trial with a lawyer for defense?"

Uncle Philip glanced at Polly. "Can you not talk sense to this husband of yours? He has a fine future ahead of him here in Washington. But to go against the President of the United States . . . "

"No," I said, "I would not be going *against* anyone. I would be defending men and hoping for justice. Every man is entitled to that right."

My uncle could not be convinced.

Neither were the judges of the Federal Court as I pleaded my case. Most of the men were appointed by President Jefferson. I wondered if I could set aside their gratitude for honesty. I hoped I could.

I did not give up. Although I did not agree with what my clients had done, I did not think they were traitors. They were men used by a shrewd manipulator. Their actions had been reckless, evil and foolish. But they were not guilty of treason.

"Our laws are carefully drawn," I reminded the judges of the Supreme Court. "You may personally think these two men, Bollman and Swartout, were wrong in what they did. I agree with you. But that is not the question. It is God's judgement that will determine such actions. We are only asked to judge the legal questions."

I studied the faces of the men who were listening. What were they thinking? Here were the judges of the highest court in the land listening to a twenty-eight year-old lawyer tell them about the law.

"Our system of justice is the friend of every free person living in this country." I went on. "A nation is only as strong as the rights of each individual citizen. You have rights, I have rights, and Erich Bollman and Samuel Swartout have rights. These rights must be protected by fair and equal justice. Not to enjoy such protection would be to destroy all that this Nation means. I put the fate of these two men in your hands and ask for justice.''

I sat down, hoping and praying I had done my best. Now it was in the minds and hearts of the justices.

''You're a wizard with words,'' Uncle Philip told me. ''Your calm delivery, your enunciation, your poise—of course, all of it is in the Key blood.''

''Of course,'' I laughed. ''But I only hope the judges agree with you.''

How long minutes seem when you are waiting for something to happen. You try to busy yourself with activity, pushing worried thoughts from your mind.

And then a thought came to me. I remembered the story of our Lord in Gethsemane. How alone He must have felt. How sad. But He prayed and was given strength.

I prayed too. I prayed for the Lord to give me the strength to accept whatever decision the judges brought. Whether Bollman and Swartout were found innocent or guilty did not seem to matter anymore. I had done my best for them. What more does the Lord and His Father, our God, ask?

The decision delighted me. Bollman and Swartout were found ''not guilty'' in the eyes of the law.

Yet I had learned an even greater lesson. Faith offers strength and courage during the most difficult times.

Family Fun

When Polly and I first came to our home on Bridge Street in Georgetown, it seemed like a mansion. There is nothing like children to reduce the size of a house.

"Will you help tie my pink ribbon?"

"Father, I need a new pair of shoes."

"Mother, Frank Jr. poked me in the eye."

All day long the sounds of children filled the neighborhood. The Keys made more than their share. They seemed able to sense when I was talking with a client in my law offices. It was then that their loudest yelps and shouts would shake the house. I was grateful for the quiet and peace within the courtroom.

Once when I came home, Frank Jr. came running down the road and met my carriage. Before I stopped, he scrambled up on the seat beside me and grabbed the reins.

"Whoa!" the boy ordered, pulling the reins to his chest. "Whoa, whoa!"

"What's happened?" I asked.

"Pa, the chickens got loose. Elizabeth forgot to close

the chicken house fence when she went for eggs this morning.''

I shook my head. ''I told you all when we got those chickens, you had to take good care of them. You'll never get them back. What if they get mixed up with the Winthrop chickens?''

Frank Jr. shook his head. ''I can tell our chickens from any others. Just walk the buggy to the house, Pa. I don't want you running over any ·of our chickens. We'll get them all back. You just wait and see.''

By nightfall, all but one of the chickens stood cackling away in the backyard. Elizabeth, Maria, and Frank Jr. were exhausted. Yet they wanted to find the one missing chicken.

''I didn't think you would find this many,'' I offered. ''Don't worry about the one you're missing.''

''We've got to find her,'' Elizabeth insisted.

''We're going to search through the neighborhood one more time,'' added Maria.

''There is no need for that,'' I answered.

Frank Jr. stood firm. ''Remember what you taught us in Sunday school, Pa? Remember the story about the shepherd who lost one lamb? He went looking for him.''

Elizabeth backed him up. ''There was that woman who lost just one of her coins too. She looked until she found it.''

I glanced over at Polly. My wife only smiled.

''All right,'' I replied. ''We will watch over your traveling chickens for one hour. But then you must be back home, with or without the missing chicken.''

Off the three of them went. Polly walked over to me, slipping her arm inside of mine.

''Someone I know is not only a fine lawyer but a fine Sunday school teacher as well,'' she teased.

Within the hour, the happy trio returned. In

Frank's arms was a wiggling chicken.

"Now, to bed with the lot of you," I ordered, my voice firm and strict.

"Thanks, Pa," the laughing threesome answered.

My work as a Sunday school teacher at St. John's brought me great joy. Being a member of the parish council gave me pleasure as well, but there was a special excitement in bringing God's word to young boys and girls who had never heard it.

"Where did people sleep in Bethlehem?" a girl might ask.

"What did people use for money long ago?" another questioner would wonder.

The questions would send me searching through the Bible and other church books. Reverend Sayrs often joined me in the search.

"You are a good teacher," the minister told me one morning. "You give us so much of your time and you give us one-tenth of your earnings as well."

I was grateful for the kind words. But in truth, my contributions seemed small indeed. After all, it was the Lord who was with us at all times and in all places.

Reverend Sayrs' death saddened us all. He had been a kind and respected leader. Yet I could not offer a message of grief when the parish council called upon me to write an inscription to hang in the church. Instead, I told the people to be glad that our minister was with the Lord.

"Here lies he now," I wrote, "yet grieve thou not for him, reader! He trusted in that love where none have ever vainly trusted."

Each passing year brought more and more people to Washington D.C. No longer were the roads filled with holes and ruts. The buildings of rich wood and fine stone graced the skyline of our capital city. It was a proud community.

But beneath the outer beauty and calm of streets and building was an uneasiness. People gathered in shops and on corners to talk about news of the world. Troubled times lay ahead. If only we could know the future.

Shadows of War

Pretty as a blossom is my little Polly
*   girl*
Knows the latest dance steps, how to
*   minuet and twirl,*
Knits her brow when angry, hangs her
*   lip when sad*
Polly Key's my loving wife, and for
*   that I'm glad!*

Her eyes sparkling with merriment, Polly laughed at my birthday poem. It was a gift she always insisted upon—a special verse written just for her. She never had to ask twice.

In truth, Polly's request led me to set aside a few hours each week for the writing and reading of poetry. I soon expanded this "quiet time" to include studying theology and ethics.

"It is too bad you could not have become a minister of faith as well as an attorney of law," Polly chided me.

"One cannot follow every path when he reaches a crossroads," I replied. "So you think I might have made a good preacher, do you?"

Polly nodded. "You do not gamble, drink or swear as so many other men. Your tastes in clothes are plain and simple. You are as good a listener as you are a speaker, yet you show no trace of vanity."

"Ah, there you are wrong. I am most conceited about the girl I married."

Polly blushed. "Oh, Frank, I only hope you are happy."

"Happy enough," I answered. "But there is so much to do and not enough time to do everything I want."

I collapsed into my favorite overstuffed chair. Polly moved behind my back, gently rubbing the temples of my head with her soft fingers. I closed my eyes and relaxed.

Polly, Polly. Always leading into conversation that she knows will soothe me.

"The schoolmaster is most pleased," I answered. "I've been asked to give speeches in behalf of free education before several groups. We've received letters from people in Pennsylvania and Maryland. It seems they've heard of our program of public education and wish to start their own."

"Perhaps we should think about sending our own brood to school," murmured Polly. "You have so much to do and—"

I took my wife's hands in my own and pulled her around so that she stood before me.

"I shall tend to the education of my own children for the time being," I stated firmly. "Public schools are just starting and need to work out their flaws. Anyway, I enjoy teaching."

Polly shook her head. "You are stubborn, Frank. You do not have many faults, but you are a bit stubborn."

I stood up and pulled Polly into my arms. "Stubborn I am, and hungry as well. Where have you hid-

den the birthday cake I smelled baking this morning?
I shall devour a giant piece.''

"You'll lose that slender frame," Polly teased.

"Never!" I promised.

I did all that I could to keep our family life cheerful and merry. The laughter of Polly and the children
was like a happy song. Often we invited guests into
our home, sharing dinner and conversation. When
James Madison became President of the United States
in 1809, his wife Dolly began entertaining often too.

"Madison has Dolly and Key has lovely Polly,"
Uncle Philip laughed, "and every party given is as
joyful as it's jolly!"

"I thought I was suppose to be the verse maker in
this family," I teased my uncle.

Uncle Philip bowed low. "Indeed, you are, my boy,
and it is a title I will not claim from you."

Laughter. Parties. Fun. How I wished that such
good times would go on forever.

But after dinner parties, when the men and women
went their separate ways for conversation, the conversation grew more somber. England had declared
war against France. English sea captains tried to stop
American ships from taking goods to France.
Sometimes American sailors were taken prisoner and
forced to serve on British ships. The American traders
were furious.

"The English have no right to control the seas,"
one of my businessmen friends remarked one evening. "The seas should be free for all to use."

"President Madison has warned the British," I
offered.

"Words are useless. The British are deaf to words.
The only language they'll listen to is gunfire!"

"Gunfire is the language of death."

I turned to the man who had spoken. It was John
Randolph, a lawyer from Virginia. We had often been

on opposite sides of arguments, but this time I agreed with him completely. I recalled my mother's quote from Ecclesiastes . . . "Wisdom is better than weapons of war."

"Would you rather have America give away our ships and our men to the British?"

John Randolph shook his head. "Agreements can be made. Contracts can be signed. A war between England and France is not the concern of the United States."

The businessman pounded his fist into his other hand. "Well, we shall see what President Madison has to say about the taking of our ships."

I feared the thinking of our leader in the White House. He was a fine scholar, a man of culture and refinement; but he was too willing to accept the advice of those around him. Many of those people were eager for war.

I began to spend more time with John Randolph. I fancied myself clever with words but I was no match for him. I visited the gallery of Congress to hear his speeches. With power and eloquence, he agrued against the United States going to war against England. Uncle Philip stood to speak against any fighting too.

I felt a kinship to John Randolph. Once, when he wrote me of doubts he had with his Christian faith, I answered him as if he were my brother:

"Men may argue ingeniously against our faith, as indeed they may against anything. But what can they say in defense of their own? I would carry the war into their own territories. I would ask them what they believe, if they said they believed anything. I think their beliefs might be shown to be more full of difficulties and liable to infinitely greater objections than the system they oppose.

"If they said they did not believe anything, you

could not, to be sure, have anything further to say to them. In that case, they would be insane, or at best ill-qualified to teach others what they ought to believe or disbelieve.''

My words seemed to help John. He found new strength and hope in his beliefs.

But as his spiritual faith grew stronger, so did the talk of war against England grow more heated in Washington. No matter how eloquently John and Uncle Philip argued in the House of Representatives, they could not rally more supporters.

In June of 1812, the votes were taken. The House of Representatives voted 79 to 49 for a declaration of war against England. The Senate voted 19 to 13 in favor of the same action.

Memories of the War of Independence still lingered with many Americans. Yet now we were at it again. I feared what the future would bring.

Attack!

"Whoa, Moonbeam. Whoa!"

As soon as my horse stopped, I slid off her back. Admiring the large brick home before me, I inhaled deeply. The fragrance of roses filled the air. Quickly I tied my horse and hurried to the door. I hoped Dr. Beanes would be home.

Ever since war had been declared, I had longed to talk with Dr. Beanes. He had been a physician during the War of Independence, and we were distantly related. Whenever the old doctor came to Washington, he visited my home in Georgetown. His conversation was always alert and enlightened.

"I do believe you enjoy your talks with Dr. Beanes more than all the other wags and wits that come here," Polly often said.

There was much truth to her observation. Although the good doctor was a Federalist and I had declared myself a Democrat, we still shared many agreements. There was little doubt that Dr. Beanes and I would share similar thoughts about the war.

"It is good to see you, young Francis," the doctor

greeted me. "Each day I seem to meet someone else who sings your praises. 'Brightest lawyer in all Washington' a man told me last week. I must confess I did not disagree."

"It is good to hear such things," I answered. "There is little other news around Washington that is as cheerful."

Slowly the doctor rose and walked to the window. He looked out at the rose bushes that clustered around his house.

"The Lord has given us such a beautiful world in which to live," said Dr. Beanes. "It is a shame that man has to make such a mess of things. How well I remember the ugliness and death of the last war. Perhaps if Madison and some of his friends had held a dying soldier in their arms, a man ripped in pieces by shells, perhaps then they might think twice about fighting . . ."

"It is said we have only a dozen warships," I said, "and a small army."

The doctor rubbed his chin. "The British fleet is always strong and their soldiers ready. Sometimes people can be too proud. We are still so young a country, just learning to crawl. Yet there are those who would have us fully grown, ready to take on any challenge."

I watched the doctor closely as he spoke. What pictures he must carry in his mind. Boston. Valley Forge. So many battlegrounds. He turned to me without warning.

"And what are your plans, Francis? I would hope and pray you do not aspire to become a soldier."

I shook my head. "I carry no such dreams."

"How is Polly and your tribe? How many are there now?"

"The good Lord has blessed us with five urchins," I laughed. "There are days when I think I would not hear the sounds of battle if they were made in Georgetown itself. You cannot imagine the noise within our home at times."

Again Dr. Beanes gazed out his window. "But the sounds of youth are welcome sounds," he said. "Be grateful for such noises. It is the sound of guns, the ugly thunder of shelling that are the sounds of ugliness and death. I would hope you would never hear those sounds."

I thought a lot about Dr. Beanes as I rode home that afternoon. Maybe, just maybe, the British, the French, and the Americans could mend their disagreements and we could all work in peace.

It was a foolish notion.

Since England controlled Canada, the British began to build up forces there. There was more and more talk of invading our neighbor to the north.

"We ought to send those British back across the

sea,'' wrote one newspaper editor in Washington.

"We cannot be cowards,'' wrote another editor. "Our reputation is at stake.''

Is that the only image we wished to carry around the world, I wondered. Did we only wish to be known as good soldiers, fine fighters? I hoped that we might be thought of as a peaceful nation, dedicated to hard work and living God's law. But those who thought as I did suffered. John Randolph lost his re-election campaign to Congress. Uncle Philip was snubbed openly by friends and associates.

My own law practice suffered too. I spent more and more time teaching my children. Gone were the days of happy parties. I found myself short tempered and irritable. I tried to hide my worries from Polly, but she knew me too well.

"Sometimes the Lord puts troubles before us to test our strength,'' she said one evening after we had put the children to bed. "We must hold on to our faith during good weather or bad.''

"We had better be having a few sunny days soon,'' I answered. "I cannot keep practicing law without clients.''

While I struggled with problems of keeping food in the pantry cabinets, America was building up a small army. Sure enough, our soldiers were sent northward to Canada. The invasion was a half-hearted effort, neither side scoring a victory.

Our invasion of Canada made the British angry. They sent raiding parties on ships up Chesapeake Bay. British soldiers landed and burned buildings. Faces in Georgetown and Washington showed fear and worry. Finally, I told Polly of the decision I had made.

"I'm going to enlist in the Army.''

For a moment, Polly was silent. Then I could see the tears forming in her eyes.

"I have to do it, love. It was different when the

fighting was on the seas or in Canada. But now the British are knocking on our door.''

"But the children—''

"They are the reason I must sign up," I answered. "I hate war and fighting, but when a man's family and home are in danger, that man has to act. George Peter is organizing a company of men. He's a good man, and we won't fight unless we have to . . . ''

The next several days were spent getting a uniform and basic military training. But before I received a fieldpiece weapon, the need for our company disappeared. The British leaders withdrew their ships from Chesapeake Bay. We had been in the service of our country for only eleven days.

Less than a year later, we were again called back into action. This time the threat was even closer to home. British Rear Admiral Cockburn led his soldiers on several inland attacks along the Maryland shores. Major Peter told me he wanted me to handle supplies.

"As our quartermaster, you'll be a lieutenant, Frank. It's a bit more pay.''

Major Peter clearly knew about my financial position. As quartermaster, I was expected to get horses, wagons and food from my neighbors and friends. I agreed to accept the position.

The food was easy to get, but horses and wagons were not donated as willingly. The farmers I talked to had a difficult problem.

"You ask for our horses, Lieutenant Key, and we would like to give them to you," one farmer told me. "We're as loyal to our country as anyone else. But you also need food. Without our horses, we cannot plow and harvest our crops.''

As a lawyer, I knew the farmers had a good case. But as an army quartermaster, I knew the powers I might have to use. The soldiers in my company had to have transportation and supplies. If we could not

get donations, we could legally take whatever we needed. It was not a task I liked to think about.

But when news came that British ships were sailing up the Potomac, our company left at once. I was
sent ahead to make sure food was waiting when the
men arrived. I followed orders, but I did not enjoy
them. My hate of war grew even deeper.

When we finally spotted enemy ships at Benedict,
we waited for raiders to land. One day went by, then
two and three. When we awakened the fourth morning, the British ships were nowhere in sight.

"They probably heard we were here," Major Peter
laughed. "They were too frightened to fight us!"

"I wanted to spill some English blood," one man
in our company shouted. "What a beautiful sight
would be soil soaked with the blood of British
soldiers."

I felt disgusted. What kind of man would enjoy killing another? It was God who allowed man to be born,
and it was God who had the right to take life away.

"It's back to Georgetown" Major Peter ordered.
"Those are our orders."

Glad I was for those orders. Off I went, a day ahead
of the company. I was happy to find food more easily
donated on the way home. It was good to find Polly
and the children waiting at home.

In the weeks that followed, there was more talk
about a future British attack. Men huddled in clusters
everywhere.

Some thought the British planned to attack
Annapolis.

Others wondered if Baltimore might be the target.

As for me, I wrote for Taney to come for a visit.
I had my own ideas of British plans.

"I'm thinking the British may strike Washington,"
I told my friend and brother-in-law. "It would throw
the Capital into wild confusion."

"President Madison doesn't seem worried about such an attack," Taney challenged.

I pounded one fist into my other open hand. "Yes, he thinks if and when an attack comes, all he will do is call out a militia. I've seen our soldiers, Roger! We are untrained and unprepared. We would have little strength against the British."

"Why did you ask me to come here to Georgetown?"

"I want you to take Polly and the children back with you. Take them to Terra Rubra where they will be out of danger."

"But will Polly go?"

"I shall tell her she must," I answered. "I do not want my family here if Washington is attacked."

I had enjoyed much success in the courtroom. I had swung stone-willed judges to my side when I argued. Words on paper came to me easily as I wrote my poetry. I was certain I possessed eloquence and wit when I presented my law cases. But no matter how I phrased my wishes, Polly stood firm.

"No, Frank, I will not leave Georgetown. My place is here with you." Her eyes flashed determination, sparks of devotion and love. "Now you may talk until the Judgement Day, but I will not leave."

Oh, Polly. How brave your spirit and will. How strong your resolve. How can I fault you for the very qualities that I love. You are loving and devoted. The Lord has truly blessed me.

No sooner had Taney left for his return to Frederick when I received word from Major Peter. Our company was ordered to re-form and be ready for active duty. British troops had landed at Benedict.

"You'll be careful, Frank?" Polly whispered.

I smiled. "I have too much to come back to," I answered. "Keep me in your prayers."

There was little doubt that the British were planning a major attack. But we did nothing but sit and wait. President Madison rode out to inspect our troops. So did Secretary of State Monroe and Secretary of War Armstrong. Each time we put on our cleanest uniforms and shined our rifles until they sparkled. It was like some foolish game.

"Why can't we attack them?" I asked Major Peter. "If we surprised them, perhaps fewer lives would be lost and we could send them scurrying for home!"

"We have our orders, Lieutenant," the Major replied.

Days crawled by. Finally, on the morning of August 24, 1814, the British made their move. They began marching toward Bladensburg, a village just outside Washington. "They're heading toward Washington, aren't they?" I asked Major Peter. It was a question that needed no answer. Of course, that's where they were going. Oh, why couldn't Polly have listened and gone to Terra Rubra?

What followed was a nightmare.

"Prepare to march!" Major Peter ordered.

No sooner were we prepared, when we were told to disassemble. Then we were ordered to ready our firearms. Again, we made ready to march. New orders came. We were told to wait.

Everyone grew anxious with worry. Why didn't we move? Were we just going to let the British take the capital, our homes and families?

"My hope is in Thee," I prayed, recalling Psalms 39:7. "My hope is in Thee."

When the Major gave the order to reassemble and march forward, he did not have to say it twice. We were ready. We advanced swiftly along the road to Washington, ready to block the enemy as they came.

But we were no match for the strong British force.

Onward the enemy soldiers came, their guns spouting death. Our troops could not hold them back.

"Retreat!" came the order over the explosions of rockets and guns.

No order was needed. Our soldiers fled in every direction. I jumped on my horse and headed for home.

Polly met me at the door as I burst through. Her frightened face told me she had heard the news.

"Will they come here to Georgetown?" she asked, fear edging her voice.

"No one knows," I answered. "But we must get the children ready to leave. We'll go to Terra Rubra at once. Have the servants pack."

"Oh, Frank," Polly burst out. "I'm not sure I—"

"There is no time, love. Now hurry."

The British wasted no time. By nightfall, they had control of Washington. As I watched out the window, a small glow appeared in the eastern sky. Larger it grew, and still larger. Tom, one of our servants, burst into the room.

"We've just received word, Master Key. The British have burned the Capitol building and the President's mansion. The President and his wife are safe though. They say Miss Dolly wouldn't go 'til there were sparks on her dress hem."

"Hm-m" I could not find words to say anything. Ever since I had come to Georgetown, I had watched Washington take shape and grow into a beautiful city. Now it was going up in flame and smoke.

By the next morning, Polly and the children were ready to leave for Terra Rubra at a moment's notice. I jumped on my horse and rode to the Montgomery Courthouse. Surely there would be news of our company. We had to send those British running!

Once more I found complete confusion. People were running around, no one in charge. When I saw Major Peter, he hurried to my side.

"Sorry, Lieutenant. No further orders." His face looked drawn, his eyes tired. "Why don't you go back to your family. You'll be notified when the men are reassembling."

"No further orders." The words drummed in my mind. How could we allow British troops to burn our Capitol, ravage our land, insult the spirit of our country? It was shameful.

Yet I felt a certain shame about myself. How could I be so eager for war? Killing, bloodshed, death—I hated all of it. Yet it seemed necessary, at least in defense of liberty and freedom.

When I arrived home, I found my friend Richard West pacing in the hallway. His clothes looked rumpled and his hand shook as it enclosed mine.

"It's Dr. Beanes," he blurted out. "The British have taken him prisoner."

I could not believe my ears. "Taken him prisoner? On what charge?"

"Well, the British had been staying in Upper Marlboro," West explained. "Although the soldiers had been ordered by their generals to leave, a few of them remained. They got drunk and became rowdy. Dr. Beanes ordered the three men arrested."

"Rightly so!" I declared.

"According to you, perhaps. But not according to the British. They had the good doctor arrested and took him aboard their flagship."

"It's outrageous! Taking an old man from his home. What can we do to get him back?"

West smiled. "I was hoping you would say that. If anyone can plead his case and get Dr. Beanes back, you can."

"But I'm still awaiting orders. General Winder is in charge of my company. We'll need permission from President Madison to board the British flagship under a flag of truce—"

"Can we get started at once, sir?"

"At once!"

Quickly we rode to the private home where President Madison had taken up residence. He was quick to grant permission for my trip, since he knew Dr. Beanes himself.

"General Winder is in Annapolis preparing our defenses. He will release you for your mission." The President dipped his quill into the bottle of ink on his desk. His hand was steady as he wrote on parchment. "You'll take this note to Colonel Skinner. He's in charge of our exchange of prisoners. I want him to accompany you."

Taking the letter from President Madison, I thanked him for his help. He gently took my arm as I left.

"These are times of war," he said quietly. "Any mission of this kind has its own dangers."

I nodded. I knew there were risks, but I tried to put them from my mind. Dr. Beanes had to be set free. That thought and that thought only burned in my head. I mounted my horse and hurried to find General Winder and Colonel Skinner.

"The Star Spangled Banner"

There was no trouble in getting cooperation for my mission. Dr. Beanes was far better known that I had thought. Everyone thought highly of the old gentleman.

"It's an outrage!" exclaimed Colonel Skinner. "The old man is guilty of nothing other than wanting his village rid of nuisances."

"I've been told Dr. Beanes is being held prisoner aboard the flagship of the British fleet," I offered.

"That would be the Tonnant," the Colonel replied. "The fleet is somewhere in the Chesapeake. We'll sail from Baltimore and find her."

Our horses seemed to sense the importance of our task. As we urged them faster, their steps quickened.

Baltimore steamed with excitement. The people knew British troops might land at any time and stage raids. There was also a chance the city could be attacked from the water. The British warships boasted long range cannon.

"The city has been readying itself for weeks," Colonel Skinner explained. "Heavy cannon are placed in position at Fort McHenry."

Made of sturdy brick and wood, Fort McHenry rested comfortably at the entrance to the Baltimore harbor. It was shaped like a star.

"Perhaps you would like to visit the fort," the colonel suggested.

"I would rather complete our mission for Dr. Beanes first," I stated.

Colonel Skinner agreed.

Once our horses were taken care of, the colonel and I hurried to the Baltimore wharf. Skinner led the way to a small, narrow craft. The crew was ready for us and we departed within an hour.

"Lieutenant Key, I fancy you'll have all your fine speaking talents tested by Admiral Cockburn. He would be better suited to leading snakes and rats than men. I have never heard a kind word spoken of the man," Colonel Skinner extended some papers wrapped in a blue ribbon. "These may be of some help."

As I untied the narrow slip of cloth, I noticed the papers were letters. Each one testified to Dr. Beanes' able and kind treatment of wounds during battle. The letters were signed by British soldiers.

"These letters can certainly do us no harm," I answered.

Colonel Skinner motioned me to the side of our vessel. He pointed across the water.

"You can see how important Fort McHenry is to the defense of Baltimore," he said.

I nodded. It was not only the fort itself which impressed me. It was the giant flag of our country . . . the largest banner I had ever seen.

"Your eyes are wide," the colonel laughed. "Yes, it is quite a flag, isn't it? It measures a full thirty by forty-two feet. A young widow named Pickersgill made it. The Commandant of the fort, Major Armistead requested a banner so large that the enemy would have no difficulty in seeing it from a distance.''

"Indeed!" I laughed. "I would think the British might be able to see that banner from the shores of their own England!"

Our ship, the Minden, smoothly sailed through the waters of the Chesapeake. But we saw no sight of the British fleet the first day out. Success was with us on the second day.

"Ship ahoy!" a lookout called. "British ship ahoy!"

As minutes slipped away, we discovered there was not only one ship on the horizon, but many. Skinner yelled up at the lookout.

"How many can you count?"

The lookout looked through field glasses from his position. "Could be thirty-five or forty of them, Sir. They are coming this way."

Quickly, our crew ran up the flag of truce. A large battleship came closer. Colonel Skinner hailed the vessel and called out our names. We were invited to come aboard.

At first, I thought Colonel Skinner might have misjudged Admiral Cockburn. He seemed friendly enough, his stomach amply filling his uniform and his hands clenching and unclenching themselves. But once I mentioned the name of Dr. Beanes, the Admiral's face reddened.

"I am planning on hanging the doctor to the yardarm of this vessel," he announced, taking a heavy swig of ale at dinner. "The man is a varmint and a pig."

I restrained myself from dousing my host with his own mug. Instead, I handed Admiral Cockburn the letters. As he read, I pleaded the doctor's case.

"Dr. Beanes is a harmless man," I began. "In truth, he may not have realized the seriousness of the action he was taking in arresting your three soldiers. He is known to treat everyone he knows with respect and kindness, perhaps much like yourself. . . "

On I went, and on further. As I spoke, I remembered how I would sometimes flatter my sister Ann to gain special favors. It had all worked well until my mother had told my sister the words from the Good Book: *He shall come in peaceably, and obtain the kingdom by flatteries.* It was Daniel 11:21, I believe. Thankfully, the admiral seemed to enjoy remarks aimed to suit his vanity.

As he read, our host's manner mellowed. The letters were passed to his other officers dining with us. Their reactions seemed positive. By the time Skinner and I left his quarters that evening, I was convinced Dr. Beanes was soon to be a free man.

My feelings proved true enough. We received word that Dr.Beanes was to be released to us.

"Now, if we can only sail away from here swiftly," Colonel Skinner said softly. "There is much movement afoot. Whispers run rampant."

I had noticed this as well. Sailors were constantly active, never stopping to look our way. I hoped the Minden could return us to Baltimore as safely as she had brought us to the Tonnant.

But as we were leaving the flagship, a British officer hurried to us.

"I'm sorry, gentleman," the Englishman said firmly. "You will be returned to your own ship at once. We will furnish you with a crew. For the time being, though, you will sail with us."

"We do not choose to remain," I answered. "Why are you detaining us?"

The officer looked at me with narrowed eyes.

"Sir, we are about to attack Baltimore. You will remain with the fleet until the battle is over."

I swallowed deeply. I felt as if this were a bad dream, a horrible nightmare from which I would soon awaken.

"But we've come to you under a flag of truce!" Colonel Skinner protested.

"You will not be harmed in any way," the officer answered. "The three of you will be taken back to your ship until the fighting is over and we have secured Baltimore."

"You sound very certain of yourself," I snapped. "What if your attack should fail?"

The British officer stared at me, his eyes revealing a total disgust. Suddenly he turned to a few of his sailors standing nearby.

"Return these men to the Minden at once!" he ordered.

The orders were obeyed. An hour later we stood on the deck of our own ship, sailing up the bay with the British fleet.

"This is outrageous!" Dr. Beanes declared. "They broke into my home and dragged me from my bed. They kept me in irons. Now they make me a witness to an attack on my own country."

I felt just as angry as the good doctor, but a sick feeling ate at my stomach as well. Here I was, a lieutenant in the United States Army, aboard an enemy ship. An attack was going to be launched against my people, my nation, and I was helpless to stop it.

Colonel Skinner cast a comforting arm around my shoulder. His eyes were misty.

"I know what you're feeling, my friend, but there is nothing we can do."

" . . . nothing we can do." The words struck a familiar chord in my memory. It brought back a vision of Grandmother Key as I read to her. It was a horrid rainy afternoon, and I could not go outside. I had wanted to explore a woods nearby and ride a horse.

"Well," Grandmother had said, "the rain is here and there is nothing we can do about it. But we can always pray together. Remember, Francis, you can always pray, even by yourself. That is always something you can do . . . "

So, on that night of September 13, 1814, I stood on board the Minden and prayed. I watched as the ships in the fleet formed halfcircles around the fort. British gunners awaited the signal to fire. When it came, the thunder of shells rumbled across the bay.

Our ship was outside of reach when the fort returned the enemy's fire. Sadly enough, the shells from the fort fell short. It was clear the British had our own troops outgunned.

Ca-boom! Boom! Ca-boom! The bombs and rockets pounded the fort. Heavy smoke from the burned powder filled the bay.

"Is the flag still flying over the fort?" Dr. Beanes asked. "I cannot see that far."

I strained to see through the smoke. Yes, the flag was still flying. Thank God it was such a huge banner.

"Yes, Doctor, it still flies."

"Let us hope it will remain flying," Colonel Skinner said softly. "If it falls, it means the fort has surrendered."

"The city will no longer be free," the doctor said. "I pray those brave men in the fort can hold out."

I watched the doctor shuffle away, disappearing into the darkness. My heart ached for him. He still carried memories of the War of Independence battles. Now he was a witness to this.

From my pocket I took an envelope. So often in the past I had jotted down a few lines for a poem which I completed later. Now I scribbled a few words and phrases. America was a land of brave and free people. The flag symbolized that freedom, that courage. The words came quickly.

My head pounded with the sound of exploding shots and shells. Waves slapped against the sides of the

Minden, raising and lowering the craft in the water. Boom! Ca-boom! The rockets lit up the sky with their glare. Again I scribbled my impressions.

I paced along the deck, aware that I was surrounded by hostile sailors. They were hoping for the fort to fall just as strongly as I prayed for it to hold. The smoke grew so thick we could no longer even see the giant banner of our country. Maryland had called upon its sons to defend that flag and our nation. I prayed for their success.

Rain began to fall. The ships moved closer to the fort. Then Fort McHenry cut loose with all its guns. Boom! Ca-boom! I coughed violently, choking on the heavy smoke.

Without warning the firing stopped. The air was still. How I longed to see the fort. Was the flag still flying? Or perhaps the stars and stripes have given way to the British banner.

"What's happened?" Doctor Beanes asked, stumbling up on deck. "Has the fort surrendered?"

"We don't know," I answered. "We can't know until sunrise."

Time crawled. We stood waiting in the darkness. My mouth felt dusty and dry. Dampness covered my body as the rain mingled with my own body moisture.

"The sun's coming up," Colonel Skinner murmured. "The dawn is breaking."

Once more I took out my envelopes. I scribbled away, noting the glow of the dawn's early light. The mist had cleared away the smoke.

"I can see it!" I exclaimed. "The flag—our flag— it's still there!"

The doctor grabbed my arm. He leaned across the railing, trying desperately to see.

"Are you sure it is *our* flag, Francis?"

"Yes, yes!" I answered. "It is ours! It's our beloved red, white and blue. May God be praised!"

My hand raced across the envelope recording what
I felt and what I was seeing. The sailors moved around
us, preparing to leave. Soon the British crew left the
ship and our own sailors took over. Joyfully, we watched the enemy ships sail away.

"They've given up," I exclaimed. "We've won!"

Within hours, the Minden was headed for the wharf
in the Baltimore harbor. The thoughts of a warm meal
and a clean bed filled my head. But there was
something I had to do first.

Once we found a room in a Baltimore inn, Doctor
Beanes and Colonel Skinner ate a hearty meal and
headed for bed. I joined them for the meal, but I asked
the innkeeper for paper, ink and quill when I went
to my room.

By the soft light of morning, I began to write. I
studied the notes I had written on the envelope. The
phrases came back to me. I hummed the melody from
an old hymn, "To Anacreon in Heaven." The uplif-
ting tune seemed to fit the joy of my verses. It sounded
good to me. Maybe others might share its strength
and we could send those British back to England. I
reread the four sheets of paper with my new poem
on them.

> O! say can you see by the dawn's early
>   light,
> What so proudly we hail'd at the
>   twilight's last gleaming?
> Whose broad stripes and bright stars,
>   thro' the perilous fight,
> O'er the ramparts we watched were so
>   gallantly streaming?
> And the rocket's red glare, the bombs
>   bursting in air,
> Gave proof thro' the night that our
>   flag was still there;

*O! say does that star spangled banner
    yet wave*
*O'er the land of the free and the home
    of the brave!*

*On the shore, dimly seen through the
    mist of the deep,*
*Where the foe's haughty host in dread
    silence reposes,*
*What is that which the breeze, o'er the
    towering steep,*
*As it fitfully blows, half conceals, half
    discloses?*
*Now it catches the gleam of the
    morning's first beam,*
*In full glory reflected, now shines on
    the steam;*
*'Tis the star spangled banner, O! long
    may it wave*
*O'er the land of the free and the home
    of the brave!*

*And where is that band who so
    vauntingly swore,*
*That the havoc of war and the battle's
    confusion*
*And home and a country, shall leave
    us no more?*
*Their blood has washed out their foul
    footstep's pollution;*
*No refuge could save the hireling and
    slave*
*From the terror of flight or in the
    gloom of the grave,*
*And the star spangled banner in
    triumph doth wave*

> *O'er the land of the free, and the*
> *home of the brave!*
>
> *O! thus be it ever when free men shall*
> *stand*
> *Between their loved home and the*
> *war's desolation;*
> *Blest with vict'ry and peace, may the*
> *Heav'n-rescued land*
> *Praise the Pow'r that hath made and*
> *preserved us a nation!*
> *Then conquer we must, when our cause*
> *it is just;*
> *And this be our motto, "In God is our*
> *trust!"*
> *And the star spangled banner in*
> *triumph shall wave*
> *O'er the land of the free and the home*
> *of the brave!*

Yes, I was happy with the song. I set the paper carefully on the table and stumbled onto my bed without removing my clothes.

Sleep came swiftly.

Prayerful Patriot

We arose early the next morning. I shared my poem with Colonel Skinner and Doctor Beanes. For several moments after I finished reading, neither man spoke. Finally, the kind doctor clutched my hand in his own.

"It's perfect, my boy. I don't know how to tell you how much I enjoyed it. You've captured all the feeling of the night and morning."

Colonel Skinner smiled. "It's a stirring poem, Frank. It sounds like a song."

"Yes, yes, I wrote it to that old tune 'To Anacreon in Heaven.' I wanted to show our pride and courage and give thanks to God. I'm calling it 'The Defence of Fort McHenry.' "

"It does all that," the doctor agreed.

"I'm going to take it to my brother-in-law Joseph Nicholson. He was second-in-command at the fort during the fighting. I want to know what he thinks of it."

"A wise thought," observed Colonel Skinner. "We wish you good fortune with 'The Defence of Fort

McHenry.' I hope it causes people to rally around our star spangled banner.''

I was grateful my poem had pleased my two friends. But I was even more thrilled at my brother-in-law's reaction.

''This is a masterpiece!'' Judge Nicholson exclaimed, setting his teacup onto the table. I've always enjoyed your poems, Frank, but this is truly magnificent. It's a song to give all Americans new faith in their country. Oh, yes, and to the tune of 'To Anacreon in Heaven' this poem you've written could give us fresh spirit and pride. It could be our victory song!''

I could not believe what I heard. ''But Joseph, do you really think it's that good?''

He leaped up from the table. ''Let's take it to the Baltimore American newspaper. We'll get them to print copies. The sooner people start singing this song, the sooner the British will hear it. We need your star spangled banner to stir us to victory.''

Our horses could not carry us fast enough as we raced through the Baltimore streets. But only a young boy named Sands was at the newspaper office.

"Can you set type?" Joseph asked.

"Uh, yes, although I've not done it often."

"Then take your time, son. But we want it today."

The boy took the poem. His eyes widened as he read. "Oh, yes, sir, I shall do my best. What a fine poem it is!''

By the late afternoon when we returned, the boy had finished the task. My name did not appear on the loose handbills the lad gave us. I was simply identified as a gentleman from Maryland.

"But you should have recognition," my brother-in-law declared.

I shook my head. "I did not write the poem for my own glory," I wrote it so others might know of the defence of Fort McHenry, of the brave soldiers and of our flag.''

I was eager to return to Polly and the children. Happily, I said goodbye to my friends in Baltimore. I took the coach home, grateful for the chance of sleep. At every stop, I listened to people as they spread the joyful news of Baltimore.

"We showed those British!" one innkeeper boasted. "The war should be over soon, I'm a-thinking."

"Have you heard the new song?" another innkeeper asked us as we ate lunch. "Some call it 'In Defence of Fort McHenry' while others call it 'The Star Spangled Banner'! It's a rousing good song."

I smiled to myself. Yes, I had heard it, I thought. Indeed I have.

I was glad Polly had finally agreed to take the children to Terra Rubra before I left Georgetown. There was always something wonderful about com-

ing back to the redlands between the good old
Monocacy River and Big Pipe Creek. It was even
more wonderful when Polly came running out to meet
me.

"Oh, Frank, I've been so worried," she whispered,
holding me close.

"I'm safe and home," I murmured.

I was suddenly deluged by hugs and kisses. Mother,
Father, the children. Each seemed eager to pull an
arm from my body as a welcome.

But later, by the fire, we watched the logs crackle
and spark. The gold and orange glow of the flames
reminded me of the shells and rockets of the attack
on Fort McHenry. As I told the family everything that
had happened, I passed around the handbills contain-
ing my song. They persuaded me to sing, and before
the night was over, we were all singing joyfully.

It was good to be with loved ones. Once more, I
thanked God for His blessings.

Trouble in Alabama

The unsuccessful attack on Fort McHenry signaled the end of the British raids on the United States. I was happy and proud to see my song printed in newspapers and periodicals. It came to carry the title "The Star Spangled Banner" more and more often.

"Beware," Polly warned me. "It is difficult to go anywhere without hearing your song. Do you plan to continue your law practice, or do you plan to write songs?"

I enjoyed my wife's teasing. "Serve the Lord with gladness," I reminded her, "and come before His presence with singing."

"Is that a line of a new song you are writing?" she asked.

I shook my head. "No, it is from the Bible, Psalms 100:2. But I confess, I appreciate the line a bit more now."

"Vanity, vanity," Polly said. "Isn't it from Ecclesiastes that 'Childhood and youth are vanity'? Perhaps thirty-four year-old attorneys who write songs should also be included . . . "

Polly, oh, Polly. What a helpmate and companion. Again and again blessing me with children, keeping my home, offering fulfillment to my life.

My law practice prospered. But in truth, it seemed I received as many requests to present speeches as I did to represent clients. People everywhere wanted to hear of our adventures aboard the Minden the night of the Fort McHenry attack. I was always introduced as the man who wrote "The Star Spangled Banner." I was treated as some kind of hero, and I was sorry for that. It was the men of Fort McHenry who deserved the recognition.

One night I stood in an auditorium in Annapolis. People asked me questions about the attack. But one man in the audience changed the topic.

"Mr. Key," he said, "I understand you have released the slaves at your homestead and within your household employ. Why is that?"

"I have long felt that man should have control over his own life," I answered. "We all have but one Master on this earth, and we are all His servants."

"But I understand you still keep slaves . . . "

"No, I do not keep them," I corrected the questioner. "They have chosen to remain in my employ. A man should have that freedom of choice. I believe this is God's wish."

When I was not arguing cases in the courtroom, giving speeches or spending time with the family, I was writing, poems and more poems. Family and friends had many requests.

Working with the church provided constant joy. In 1819, I wrote a hymn that was well received. I felt a special pride when the voices of St. John's blended in song.

> *Lord, with glowing heart I'd*
> *praise thee*
> *For the bliss thy love bestows,*

*For the pardoning grace that
    saves me
And the peace that from it
    flows;
Help, O God, my weak
    endeavor;
This dull soul to rapture raise;
Thou must light the flame or
    never
Can my love be warmed to
    praise.*

*Praise, my soul, the God that
    sought thee
Wretched wandr'er, far astray;
Found thee lost, and kindly
    brought thee
From the paths of death away;
Praise with love's devoutest
    feeling,
Him who saw the guiltborn fear,
And the light of hope revealing,
Bade the bloodstained cross
    appear.*

*Lord, this bosom's ardent feeling
Vainly would my lips express
Low before thy footstool
    kneeling,
Deign thy suppliant's prayer to
    bless;
Let thy grace, my soul's chief
    treasure,
Love's pure flame within me
    raise;
And since words can never
    measure,*

Let my life show forth thy
praise. Amen.

In 1829, Andrew Jackson became President of the United States. I was delighted. He had been a general in the War of 1812. Soon after his inauguration, President Jackson invited me to his office.

"Frank, I want you to serve as the United States District Attorney of the District of Columbia," he told me. "There are many legal matters here in the nation's capital. I think you are the man who can handle the job."

I was grateful for the President's confidence. No sooner had I accepted when I learned that Roger Taney had also been appointed to a top government position. He was named as a judge to the United States Supreme Court.

"Our country is in a sad situation when the two of us are needed," Taney joked. "But I'll do my best."

"As will I," I replied.

Polly continued to be my faithful companion. The Lord blessed us with children eleven times. Three of them He took back with Him. Just as we had shared happy moments, we shared our grief. If ever I felt a need for the Lord's strength, it was during those times of loss. I wondered what people without faith did when they suffered the loss of a loved one. The thought of our children being with the Lord sustained Polly and I through our saddest moments. I thought of the words from Matthew: "Then were there brought unto Him little children, that He should put His hands on them, and pray." This was my vision— my children seated at the foot of my beloved and holy Jesus.

In 1833, President Jackson called me to his office. He sat behind a large oak desk, his lean and long face looking haggard. He shuffled a sheath of papers and he looked across at me.

"Frank, I need your help. We've got a big problem in Alabama and I'm afraid it could get worse." The President raced a trembling hand through his thick white hair. "I'd like you to go there. We need to settle this matter peacefully."

"I'll do everything I can."

As I rode in the coach to Alabama, I studied the background of the problems in Alabama. The Creek Indians had given a large parcel of land to the United States government. In return for this land, the Creek tribe was promised land for their homes. When the Indians went to settle on their new land, people living there refused to leave. Government soldiers tried to move them. Fighting broke out.

I was not looking forward to the welcome that might be waiting for me. But I was happily surprised. As my coach rolled into the town of Mobile, I heard a familiar tune.

> O! say can you see by the dawn's
>   early light
> What so proudly we hail'd at the
>   twilight's last gleaming . . .

The band played loudly as I descended from the coach. It was as warm a welcome as I could have received.

But the warmth soon faded. As I met with the Indians, the soldiers, the settlers and Alabama officials, I found tension and angry feelings.

"The United States broke promises," one Indian chief told me at our first meeting. "We have no home, no place to go."

"We settled the land and built our homes," one of the leaders of the opposing side said. "Will you take what we have worked for?"

Day after day we held meetings. Talk, talk, talk. Yelling, arguing, discussing.

I was grateful to Governor Gayle for his kind invitations to visit him at the Governor's Mansion. He and his wife liked poetry and music. Over dinner we shared spirited conversation, far removed from the struggle to settle the disagreement.

"Will you read to us, Mister Key?" one of the Gayle children asked after we had eaten one evening. "All of us like to hear your voice."

"So, you're tired of your father's voice, is that it?" the Governor laughed.

"No, but we can hear that voice anytime," came the answer.

I agreed to read. Once more it was a delight having cheerful young faces surrounding me. It reminded me of the nights with my own children. Where do the happy years fly, I wondered.

Slowly, the Indian leaders and the settlement leaders began to come together. Compromises were made in the dispute. Everyone got something he wanted, but no one got everything.

"Such is the way of life," one Indian chief said as he signed the final agreement of peace.

How true those words sounded. Six weeks it had taken us to learn something we all had known before. But at least the guns were quiet and a fresh understanding was achieved. Eagerly I returned to Polly.

Harvest Time

"Hurry, Grandpa, can't you ride any faster?"

I watched my grandson, John, press his horse faster. He disappeared along one of the trails in the woods behind Terra Rubra. I was content to dawdle, enjoying the fresh July air. Anyway, it hardly seemed dignified for an old man of sixty-two to try to keep up the pace of his ten-year-old grandson. It was not that I felt the years hanging heavy, but a man must slow a few of his steps now and then.

The wind stirred the trees a bit, dancing lightly among the leaves. It was always good to return to Terra Rubra each summer. Life in Washington was so crowded, so busy. Whenever Ann and Taney came to dinner, we talked about our eagerness to return to the old homestead.

"It is still a part of us," Ann laughed often. "Did we always cherish it as we do now?"

I nodded. "Always. How many times I saw you with the reddish layer of dust covering you like an extra skin."

"*You* should talk, Francis Scott Key! Father sent

you to the creek many a time to wash off the dirt.''

Indeed he had, indeed he had. I often missed Father and Mother. But Terra Rubra was alive with the squeals and shouts of youngsters at play. There was always a grandchild underfoot.

The years had been good to us. President Jackson had appointed Taney to be Chief Justice of the Supreme Court. After giving up my position as Attorney General, I devoted more of my time to the church and the community.

In the spring of 1841, I felt a sudden desire to travel west. Each day brought stories of pioneers traveling beyond the mountains.

"Do you feel like making a journey?" I asked my son Philip.

"When do we leave?" he asked me.

It was a delightful journey. We rode until our bodies felt bound to our saddles. Farms dotted the countryside where no families had ever lived before. Villages and towns seemed to be springing up everywhere.

" 'Tis indeed the land of the free and the home of the brave," Philip reminded me. "These pioneers are a rough, adventuresome lot."

"They've a spirit of America inside of them," I agreed. "It's surely a good land that pulls them on and gives them courage. Let's hope God rewards them for their efforts."

Each time Polly and I returned to Washington, we discovered new buildings and new people. Sometimes I feared the government would become too powerful. But I liked what President Van Buren had to say: "The less government interferes with private pursuits, the better for the general prosperity." Amen, I thought. A good and noble thought.

One afternoon, I set aside my papers in the law of-

fice and took a fresh piece of paper. I dipped my pen
and began to scribble a few lines:

> *Polly, dear Polly, with smile so sweet*
> *Your hair shines like sunbeams, I kneel*
> *   at your feet*
> *And thank my dear God for a*
> *   wonderful wife*
> *Who has shared golden moments, and*
> *   comforted strife.*

She laughed when I gave it to her that evening. But
it was a laugh of love, a kind and winsome sound that
brought joy to my heart.

"Always the same Francis," she whispered across
the table. "How I love you."

The next summer we returned to Terra Rubra.
Since it had been such a good planting in the spring,
I chose to remain for the fall harvest. Never had the
crops looked so alive, so rich and full.

But the winter set in early, chasing away our harvest
crew before their job was done. It did not matter.
Terra Rubra had long ago stopped bringing in any
good harvests.

"I could make a good case for selling the place,"
Taney teased me often. "It only drains your
pocketbook."

"No one could pay me enough to cause me to sell
Terra Rubra," I answered.

Shortly after we celebrated Christmas on the beloved homestead, I was summoned to Baltimore. I did
not welcome the journey as a cold had settled within
my chest. But a friend needed help. I bade Polly
farewell and departed.

My fears of the journey were justified. Never had
I felt the cold air so keenly. But the coach rolled
smoothly, so smoothly I was taken with the urge to
write.

I have been a base and groveling thing,
And the dust of earth my home,
But now I know that the end of my woe,
And the days of my bliss is come.
Then let them like me,
Make ready their shrouds
Nor shrink from the mortal strife,
And like me they shall sing,
As to heaven they spring,
Death is not the end of life.

A worthy effort, I felt, especially in my condition. My daughter in Baltimore did not agree.

"Father, it's not like you at all," Elizabeth exclaimed. "Why, it's all so sad and morbid. What is this talk of shrouds? I won't hear of you thinking of such things."

I took Elizabeth's hands into my own.

"It is not a sad poem, my loving daughter. It is

one of the most joyful poems I have ever written. It is written with the same feeling I had so many years ago while I watched Fort McHenry being attacked. It is a poem of celebration, of glory and hope.''

''What joy and hope is there in a poem that speaks of life's end?'' Elizabeth demanded. ''You would have me happy when you hint of your own death?''

''Ah, but did you not hear the final line? Death is *not* the end of life. It is but a beginning. Our Lord Jesus died so that we might enjoy eternal life with Him in heaven. I pray that there is a place for me in His kingdom.''

Elizabeth smiled, brushing away a tear that trickled down her cheek.

''Of course, Father,'' she whispered. ''Now I understand. I only hope I am as ready for the next life as you are.''

I nodded. ''If we put our faith in God, and live our lives accordingly, we shall all be ready.''

EXTRA

Baltimore Sun

Maryland's

Largest Daily Newspaper

1¢

Texas wants to become a State! (see page 2)

January 11, 1843

Death Takes Writer of "Star Spangled Banner"

Francis Scott Key

President John Tyler leads nation in mourning the death of Francis Scott Key.

Francis Scott Key passed into the arms of his loving Savior when he died today.

Many leaders of our Federal government grieve at the passing of this noted Maryland leader.

Daniel Webster noted that Key was (see page 4)

His famous poem leaves his mark on Americans for all ages.

"O! say can you see by the dawn's early light, what so proudly we hail'd at the twilight's last gleaming?

(see page 3)

BIBLIOGRAPHY

Brown, Marion Marsh. *Broad Stripes and Bright Stars.* Philadelphia: The Westminster Press, 1955.

Filby, P. W. and Howard G. *Star Spangled Books: Books, Sheet Music Newspapers, Manuscripts and Persons Associated with the Star Spangled Banner.* Baltimore: Maryland Historical Society, 1972.

Georgiady, N. P. *Our National Anthem.* Chicago: Follett Publishing Company, 1960.

Key, Francis Scott. *Star Spangled Banner.* New York: Thomas Crowell and Company, 1966.

Miller, Natelie. *Story of the Star-Spangled Banner.* Chicago: Children's Press, 1965.

Patterson, Lillie. *Francis Scott Key.* Champaign, Illinois: Garrard Publishing Company, 1963.

Smith, Francis Scott Key. *Francis Scott Key.* Washington, D.C.: Key-Smith and Company, 1911.

Sonneck, Oscar G. *Report on the Star Spangled Banner and Hail Columbia.* New York: Dover, 1972.

Spier, Peter. *The Star-Spangled Banner.* Garden City, New York: Doubleday & Company, Inc., 1973.

Stevenson, Augusta. *Francis Scott Key.* Indianapolis/New York: Bobbs-Merrill Company, Inc., 1960.

INDEX

SOWER SERIES

ATHLETE
Billy Sunday, Home Run to Heaven
by Robert Allen

BUSINESSMAN
Clinton B. Fisk, Defender of the Downtrodden
by W. F. Pindell

EXPLORERS AND PIONEERS
Christopher Columbus, Adventurer of Faith and Courage
by Bennie Rhodes

HOMEMAKERS
Abigail Adams, First Lady of Faith and Courage
by Evelyn Witter
Susanna Wesley, Mother of John and Charles
by Charles Ludwig

HUMANITARIANS
Jane Addams, Founder of Hull House
by David Collins
Florence Nightingale, God's Servant at the Battlefield
by David Collins
Teresa of Calcutta, Serving the Poorest of the Poor
by D. Jeanene Watson
Clara Barton, God's Soldier of Mercy
by David Collins

MUSICIANS AND POETS
Mahalia Jackson, Singer for God
   by Evelyn Witter
Francis Scott Key, God's Courageous Composer
   by David Collins

SCIENTISTS
George Washington Carver, Man's Slave Becomes God's
   Scientist, by David Collins
Samuel F.B. Morse, Artist with a Message
   by John Hudson Tiner
Johannes Kepler, Giant of Faith and Science
   by John Hudson Tiner
Isaac Newton, Inventor, Scientist, and Teacher
   by John Hudson Tiner
The Wright Brothers, They Gave Us Wings
   by Charles Ludwig

STATESMEN
Robert E. Lee, Gallant Christian Soldier
   by Lee Roddy
Abraham Lincoln, God's Leader for a Nation
   by David Collins
George Washington, Man of Prayer and Courage
   by Norma Cournow Camp